UNDERSTANDING EVERYDAY EXPERIENCE

Series Editor: Laurie Taylor

MIKE HEPWORTH
and
MIKE FEATHERSTONE

Surviving
Middle Age

BASIL BLACKWELL · OXFORD

First published 1982
Basil Blackwell Publisher Limited
108 Cowley Road
Oxford OX4 1JF
England

British Library Cataloguing in Publication Data

Hepworth, Mike
   Surviving middle age. — (Understanding
   everyday experience)
   1. Middle age — Psychological aspects
   I. Title II. Featherstone, Mike III. Series
   305.2'4   HQ1059.4

   ISBN 0-631-12751-8
   ISBN 0-631-12955-3 Pbk

Typesetting by Cambrian Typesetters
Farnborough, Hants
Printed in Great Britain by the Blackwell Press
Guildford, London, Oxford, Worcester

Contents

Acknowledgements   vii

Preface by Laurie Taylor   ix

Foreword   xi

1   Becoming Middle Aged   1

2   The Menopause   19

3   The Male Menopause   29

4   The Mid-Life Crisis   40

5   Changing Images of Middle Age   54

6   The Hollywood Ideal   69

7   Looking Good and Feeling Great I: 90
    Fitness and Exercise

8   Looking Good and Feeling Great II: 110
    Slimming and Cosmetic Surgery

9   New Sex Lives for Old   137

10 New Identities for Old   154

Bibliography   178

The Mid-Life Questionnaire   191

Index   201

Acknowledgements

The authors and publisher are grateful to the following for permission to reprint extracts from publications: W. H. Allen & Co. Ltd and Candy Enterprises for *Lovers and Gamblers* by Jackie Collins; the American Anthropological Association for 'Body Ritual among the Nacirema' by Horace Miner, *American Anthropologist*, 58; Dewynters Ltd in association with the National Dairy Council for *The Easy Guide to Everyday Fitness and Successful Jogging* by F. Lawrence; the Executors of the Estate of Helena Gourielli for *The Art of Feminine Beauty* by Helena Rubinstein; Harrap Limited for *The Human Face* by John Brophy; Hutchinson Books Limited for *Saxby for God* by Richard Haley; Frederick Muller Ltd for *The Male Menopause* by Derek Bowskill and Anthea Linacre; New English Library for *Fifty* by Seymour Kern; Jerry Rubin and M. Evans & Co., Inc. for *Growing (Up) at Thirty-Seven* by Jerry Rubin, copyright © 1976 by Jerry Rubin, reprinted by permission of M. Evans & Co., Inc., New York, NY 10017; Weidenfeld & Nicholson Ltd and A. D. Peters & Co. Ltd for *The Ice Age* by Margaret Drabble.

Preface

It's nearly two years since I joined my local health club. For the first six months I was along there three times a week, riding bicycles into the ground, running no further than the spot on which I stood, lifting and pushing and pulling metal weights which with a callous click simply reassumed their initial position after my sweating efforts had temporarily displaced them.

I noticed muscles beginning to sprout like gooseberries at the back of my legs and the top of my arms. This was the way to give new meaning to life, the key to a vigorous and productive middle age. And somehow I managed to keep the absurdity of it all at bay: only told friends the barest details or beat their cynicism to the draw with a quick self-deprecating joke: 'Watch out or you'll get sand kicked in your face.'

It took me time to realize that the damn weights were interfering with almost every other aspect of my life. I had become more interested in putting two inches on my biceps than in food, music or politics. I was also permanently tired — something which wasn't helped when a colleague pointed out that my second-floor health club was located directly above a business which described itself as *The Tyre and Exhaust Centre*.

Hepworth and Featherstone were the last straw. Their gently ironic account of how this new image of middle age had spread itself over the old comfortable version, and of the extremes to which its devotees had taken it, was quite enough to make me feel that there might be other things to middle age than trying to look ten years younger.

Not that they recommend any course of action. Their aim is to understand the experience of middle age rather than propose a formula for its enhancement. This is in line with the central aim of this new series which seeks to show that a whole range of experiences — sexual anxieties, feelings of loneliness and loss, of physical disability or incompetence, of growing up, coping with middle age and ageing — are at some time or another, and with varying degrees of intensity, aspects of all our lives. That is, they are not necessarily 'problems', matters for medication or treatment, or for treatises and textbooks by doctors and psychiatrists. Instead, the books in this series set out to 'reclaim' some of these experiences from the specialists and return them to the everyday world, and in that way demonstrate that they are far more manageable than they might otherwise have seemed.

Hepworth and Featherstone have not only achieved this aim, they have done so with admirable style and precision.

Laurie Taylor

Foreword

This book began one evening in the bar of a country pub not a thousand miles from a small market town in the North of England. As usual, our drinks were served by an amiable barman whose teeshirt stretched almost flamboyantly across his expansive belly. On this occasion, however, his complacency was badly shaken when some of his friends in the corner began to make humorous remarks about his generous proportions and the vast benefits he could derive from jogging, slimming, and even, if he was lucky, a more rigorous sex life.

It occurred to us that this was by no means an isolated incident but a reflection of a more general shift in attitudes towards 'middle-age spread' and other outward signs of physical ageing which had probably been either ignored or taken for granted in the past. We had for some time been collecting material for a study of the 'mid-life crisis' and returned to our press cuttings, academic notes, and interview transcripts with renewed interest. There we found abundant evidence of a new image of middle age: one in which the changes which the passage of time brings to our faces and our figures are compared unfavourably with idealized standards of perpetual youth, fitness, and beauty. As such it is an image which increasingly applies to both sexes. Women have, of course, always been under pressure to conserve their 'looks' — to make the most of their appearance — and men also are now urged to spend more and more time grooming, preserving, and 'shaping up' their bodies, especially as they pass into 'the middle years'. Our book is therefore simply an attempt to map out the contours of this new imagery, to trace it to its sources, and to draw attention to the kind of influence it can exercise over the ways in which both men and women experience middle age in everyday life.

Our thanks are due not only to our anonymous barman but also to all the other people — far too numerous to mention — who have, often unwittingly, helped us with our enquiry. In particular we wish to thank Laurie Taylor and John Davey for their encouragement, constructive criticism, and patient editing. Special thanks too to Jill Averell for her excellent typing; and last — but by no means least — to Edna and Marian for allowing us to go to the pub in the first place.

1

Becoming Middle Aged

'You're as old as you feel', the old saying optimistically proclaims, yet however much we try to remain young at heart, as we approach a 'certain age' bodily betrayals conspire to remind us of our decline. Middle age is the time when we first become conscious of the visible signs of the ageing process and the ravages which time has worked. Jokes on this theme abound: 'How do you know you're middle aged? — It's the time when you can't turn the TV set off or your au pair girl on.' Another, which appeared in the agony column of *The New York Post* runs: 'Dear Abby: when would you say a person has reached middle age? Forty and Curious.' 'Dear Forty: When he (or she) climbs out of the bathtub and is glad to find the full-length mirror all steamed up.'

In a youth orientated society the awareness of middle age is related to the way in which we react to these visible signs of ageing. They have become significant to us because they open up the prospect of a change in the attitude of others towards us, the possibility that others will no longer appreciate our true self, but will henceforth perceive us through a false and unwelcomed appearance.

In his book *The Human Face*, the artist John

Brophy points to the difficulty of becoming reconciled to a changed appearance:

> I am forty-five: middle aged. I do not yet know what it is to feel old. Physically I am strong and healthy, though short of exercise at this late stage of the war. When I look in the mirror I see white hairs above my ears: a damnable injustice, for I know plenty of men of my own age without any. My face is still fresh complexioned, and not so plump as it was a few years back. But I cannot deny that it is the face of a man — how do they call it in magazine stories — no longer in the first flush of youth. These are the indisputable facts. They ought to be deeply impressed on my consciousness. But they are not. Unless I bend my mind to it, I think of myself still as a youngster. In my casual assumptions I class myself with men round about thirty. I think of them as contemporaries. I talk to them as to contemporaries. Against the background of most of my thoughts, forty-five is a venerable age, and remote from me. It is not I who have attained that undesirable beacon, but my face and my silly white hairs. If I could disown them I would.

We spend, it is often said, a quarter of our lives growing up and three-quarters growing old. Consequently the fact that others see us as older often comes as an unpleasant surprise. Although age is one of the most common means of social classification we are most reluctant to apply it to ourselves and are pleased when those around us express disbelief in our chronological age: 'I'd never have believed you were as old as that!' or second best, 'You certainly don't look your age!' As we get older, wrote the columnist Katharine Whitehorn, the trouble is that we go on feeling the same inside: 'It's just that your body doesn't fit any more, like clothes that have shrunk — no, grown — in the wash.'

The older we become the more the wrinkled face seems to be an unwelcome façade which cruelly hides the real person underneath and no longer seems capable of expressing our true self:

> I was in my sixties but my body and mind were still youthful — yet my face looked wrinkled, sagging, and old. I wanted a youthful face to match my limber body. . . . I now face the day with an eager new sense of joy. People say I seem much more vivacious. . . . I used to be just as bright, but my wrinkles covered up the sparkle.

or,

> I'm sixty-seven but I feel vital — anywhere from forty-five to fifty-five, and I resent being bound by the arbitrary measurement of time. . . . I have an appetite for life.

Chronologically, ageing is simply a matter of living to the end of our allotted span; broadly speaking, the biblical three score years and ten. But the process of growing old is complicated by the fact that there are really two kinds of ageing: biological and social. The natural physical changes we associate with ageing are evaluated according to social norms which place a high premium on youthful energy and beauty. Some years ago the *Observer Magazine* compared a photograph of Cary Grant, who was then 64, with a picture

3

of one of his contemporaries, the Archbishop of Canterbury. In contrast with Cary Grant's lean, square-jawed face and spare physique, the Archbishop was portly, lined, and almost bald with a fringe of venerable white hair. 'What', the article asked, showing whose side it was on, 'keeps one person in youthful good looks while another matures more obviously?' Whether we like it or not, ageing is judged as much by facial and bodily appearances as by any other change. As one social worker put it, 'Fewer people would be in nursing homes if the mirror didn't tell them they had grown old.' Margaret Drabble vividly captures this state of affairs in her novel, *The Ice Age*:

Slowly, Alison Murray rose to her feet, shut the curtains, and crossed to the wardrobe mirror. Slowly, she inclined her face towards her face. The harsh unshaded light fell without mercy. Yes, there were wrinkles. At last, after years of grace, there were wrinkles. There would be more. There was strain round the eye, the mouth, the nose. The neck was slightly ringed. Rings, dark and grave, lay also beneath the eyes: dark red, weary. She bared her teeth at herself: yes, her gums were receding, slightly, they were creeping back in distaste from her too-large, too old, nicotine-stained teeth. Her face felt stiff; it woke stiff, took all day to soften, then stiffened again each evening. Her hair was touched with grey: she had always admired young women with grey hair, with white streaks in the black, had not minded her genetic inheritance: but a young woman with grey hair was one thing, an old woman with grey hair another. Meditatively, she untied her wrap, and stared at her body. There it was, source of so much

4

pleasure, so much self-congratulation. And still lovely: hardly a mark upon it, hardly a sign of wear, the body of a young woman. But for how long, she said to herself, panic beating noisily in her ears: for how much longer? When will it collapse? Will it collapse overnight, like Dorian Gray? It is unnaturally preserved already, as it was unnaturally endowed in the first place. When will I cease to be able to look at myself naked in the mirror? And God, O God, what then, what then will I do?

Not infrequently that ubiquitous piece of household equipment, the mirror, is an important reminder of the passing years. Barry Norman's novel *A Series of Defeats* opens with the central character Henry Tyson carefully examining his face in the bathroom mirror: 'Not a bad face really; a little puffier, a little plumper than it had been a few years back. Ah, but naturally. He had been young then.'

None of this would matter very much if we didn't live in a society in which personal appearance plays such an important role. Not only are we confronted by the image which stares back at us from the mirror, but we cannot avoid countless stylized media images of the face and body. Images invite comparisons, uncomfortable reminders of what we are not, what we might have been, and what with effort we might still become. In his cultural history of the human body Kern remarks:

> Ours is an age obsessed with youth, health and physical beauty. Television and the dominant visual media, churn out persistent reminders that the lithe and graceful body, the dimpled smile set in an attractive face, are the keys to happiness, perhaps even its essence.

A cultural context in which any tendency to accept the visible signs of ageing: the wrinkles, sagging flesh, middle-aged spread, thinning hair, etc, runs the danger of being interpreted as an outer reflection of an unworthy self, signs of low self-esteem and even moral weakness. As Berger and Berger comment:

> To be youthful, to be healthy and to be full of vital energies, is widely looked upon not simply as the happy condition of those favoured by nature with these qualities, but in some way a moral duty for *everyone*. Consequently to be old, to be ill or to be facing death appears not only as misfortune but in some fashion a moral failure.

The media have played an important role in creating and maintaining this moral climate which challenges the view that the body naturally and inevitably runs down with age. With the help of the ever-expanding range of slimming, health food, fitness and cosmetic aids and techniques the signs of ageing can be held at bay and the benefits of a youthful appearance enjoyed deep into the middle years. The estimation of our worthiness as a person thus becomes more dependent on the visible signs of the effort we have put into maintaining our face and figure. Even a writer like Katherine Whitehorn who can adopt a rational and progressive attitude towards the old is disconcerted by the façade of ageing. After interviewing Simone Signoret in 1978 she expressed her unhappiness over the actress's rejection of cosmetic aids. She found Signoret:

> a stout granny with a gravelly voice and rough grey hair, her skin brown and leathery, the bags under

her eyes. Great heavens, I thought, she's only 57, what has she done to her face? . . . I think we all *say* that it is noble not to care about your looks, not to mind how old people think you are; but which of us, honestly, wouldn't swap for a younger mask if we could?

According to Shirley Conran, only one of the contemporary writers on the middle years (in this case for women), most of us shrink from the idea of middle age as if it were leprosy. We don't, she says, think twice about using the phrase to describe someone else but it is shattering to have the label applied to ourselves. This apprehensive attitude towards middle age emerged recently in the 'might as well be dead' special; a new way to celebrate your fortieth birthday for which caterers supply a special punch called 'embalming fluid' and a coffin and hearse attended by two black-coated flunkeys.

In the not-too-distant past it was women who feared the loss of their 'looks' the most. Simone de Beauvoir's gloomy and exhaustive analysis of ageing in Western society asserts:

I never came across one single woman, either in life or in books, who has looked upon her own age cheerfully. In the same way no one ever speaks of 'a beautiful old woman'; the most one might say would be 'a charming old woman'. Some 'handsome old men' may be admired, but the male is not the quarry.

Times however are changing and men are becoming increasingly preoccupied with fashion, cosmetics and grooming, and the presentation of a youthful appearance. Charley Blanke is the hero of Seymour Kern's novel *Fifty — The Story of Man's Dilemma at Attaining Middle Age*. It opens with Charley waking early after his fiftieth birthday party:

As he lay, unable to sleep, he felt like one who had stumbled upon feverish activities — a saturnalia — only to waken and find he was attending his own wake. To hell with it. So he was fifty. Well, he didn't feel like it and sure didn't look it. Julian, last night, and Hy Golden, both younger, at least two years maybe three, and what do they look like Julian's lids so puffed and crêped his eyes always appear to be fighting to see through. Hy hasn't fine wrinkles any more, but deep lines all over, parenthesis and exclamation marks. And a lot of others too. When it came to his own measurements, one-fifty, never a pound more, and, on five feet nine, it looked good. Forty chest, a little arse, and thirty-two waist; go beat it.

Or take Al King, pop-star of Jackie Collins's *Lovers and Gamblers*, one of the only novels where it is possible for the characters to appear in an 'advanced state of nakedness'. As the story opens Al is studying his nakedness in a full-length mirror and he *can* bear the sight of himself because:

A week at a health farm had done him the world of good. The slight paunch he had suspected was gone, his stomach was flat as a pancake. Forty push-ups a day helped there. He turned sideways. Pretty good. The body was in fine shape. Lean, tanned, hairy, masculine. Al allowed himself a pleased smile, and leaned forward to study his face. Everything seemed in order . . .

8

Yes, he still looked pretty goddam good.

In fact he looked better than ever. The recent operation to remove the bags under his eyes had been an unqualified success, and the new teeth-capping job was excellent.

Changes in the face are especially significant because of the central role it plays in social life. We are taught to search the faces of others for clues to character and inner life. During the course of every-day interaction the face is therefore one of the main vehicles for communicating social identity. It is a personal symbol which is groomed and stylized according to the fashion of the times to convey a particular impression. As we grow older the skin loses elasticity and becomes susceptible to freckles and liver spots. Noticeable wrinkling — a natural process partly produced through facial activity — begins in our twenties when the first lines appear under the eyelids and the first traces of 'crows' feet' can be seen. By our thirties there are signs of what we ambiguously call 'personality lines' and the muscles of the face begin to sag. Skin lines, neck lines and general folding and pouching of the skin become more obvious, a process which continues inexorably through our forties, fifties, sixties and seventies, by which time our faces, if nature has been allowed to run its course, are covered with a network of tiny lines, the nose having become more prominent and the head smaller and bonier.

In a society in which people are usually fully clothed it is, of course, the face which most clearly advertises the passage of time. But throughout this century there has been a growing consciousness of the image and appearance of the human body. Even for the vast majority of us who are not film stars, celebrities, or models, body care and grooming take up a significant part of our day. A detailed history of the evolution of the mirror is still to be written but no one can deny its central role in human affairs and the equally strategic position of the bathroom in almost every household. Indeed, one sign of worldly success is to have two, three, or four etc bathrooms, showers, and water closets. This situation has reached its most extreme form in the States. Horace Miner's celebrated spoof essay 'Body Ritual among the Nacirema' (American spelled backwards) captures the extent to which cleanliness has passed beyond godliness and simple health care:

> While much of the people's time is devoted to economic pursuits, a large part of the fruits of these labours and a considerable portion of the day are spent in ritual activity. The focus of this activity is the human body, the appearance and health of which loom as a dominant concern in the ethos of the people. . . . The fundamental belief underlying the whole system appears to be that the human body is ugly and that its natural tendency is to debility and disease. Incarcerated in such a body, man's only hope is to avert these characteristics through the use of the powerful influence of ritual and ceremony. Every household has one or more shrines devoted to this purpose.

We can add that since Miner wrote these words another shrine seems to becoming the focus of ritual activity among the affluent: the gymnasium. While the celebrity lifestyle demands the services of a fully equipped gymnasium and qualified instructor, the less affluent make do with the exercise cycle, the Bull-

10

worker, the weight-training kit or yoga mat in the corner of the bedroom. The widespread popularity of the outdoor 'Californian' lifestyle has seen the emergence of leisure clothes which fit close to the human form and which consequently render the disguises and supports sculpturing the middle-aged body in former years impractical. The body on display must not just give the appearance of slimness and youthful firmness of muscle, it must actually possess these qualities. Nowhere is this premium on a slim bronzed body so apparent as in that modern playground the beach: a place of unbuttoned relaxation where everything is really hanging out, where the awkwardness of the surplus flesh which often comes with middle age can really let us down. Thus cleaniness, health care, fitness, are becoming increasingly associated with the presentation of an acceptable cosmeticized public appearance. At a point in the life cycle when they have to start to adjust to the bodily changes of the ageing process the middle aged are particularly susceptible to the promise of youthful renewal claimed by body-maintenance techniques.

It is rare indeed to hear the physical changes which accompany the middle years spoken of in a complimentary way. And visible physical changes are associated with changes in character: the transition from a youthful to a middle-aged person. Thus A. Alvarez's description of the protagonist of his novel *Hunt* sums up the situation exactly:

> A rather high complexion and in the foxy brush of hair, russet and black, the first streaks of grey. Something heavy about him: about the paunch, about the mind. Heavy and uneasy. The beginnings of middle age.

In sharp contrast, those who have withstood the anticipated ravages of time are approached with a mixture of admiration and envy as the following exchange in Haley's *Saxby for God* between the youthful Esther Moore and her middle-aged lover Bob Saxby clearly shows:

It's because your looks haven't changed much. You're Dorian Gray, Bob, aren't you? You look the same as you did then and you still sound as if you care. But somewhere there's an attic with a portrait of you, and the face is slowly getting cold and evil and hard with all the vile things you've done to get power.

Esther tells Bob she has seen Maggie, who she knows was the love of his youth:

By chance. I wouldn't have noticed her, but she was wearing the sort of clothes women wore in the 'fifties. Women sometimes do that, you know, go on wearing clothes that remind them of when they were happy. The clothes made me look at her face. She was fat and shapeless, but I knew it was her. She's married to a fat bald-headed little man, Bob, and she wears old-fashioned clothes and her eyes are dull.

With certain honourable exceptions, our attitudes towards ageing are negative. Despite all the evidence that old age is not for the majority a time of senility and sharp decline, the popular stereotype links the visible changes which ageing brings with physical infirmity, mental deterioration, incompetence, inefficiency, sexual impotence, unhappiness, isolation, and obsolescence. Old age has even been defined as an 'incurable disease' and the elderly themselves not infrequently observe that they are 'suffering' from old age. The story is told of Somerset Maugham, one of the richest authors in the world, who at his eightieth birthday party remarked 'There are many virtues in growing old', followed by a long pause '. . . I'm just trying to think what they are.' Generally speaking people tend to think less of themselves as they grow older and this is not due simply to the frailties of old age. A variety of studies show that changes in face and figure reflected in the mirror and the reactions of day-to-day contacts have an important part to play. Confrontation with the stereotypes of ageing can therefore produce feelings of anxiety, depression and desperation during the middle years when the sense of time running out first takes root.

Time has, of course, always governed human life but our present-day approach to it has its own particular drawbacks. As technology has advanced, the precise measurement and utilization of time has come to be one of our most prized skills. The increasingly sophisticated division of time makes us ever more sensitive to the Western notion that it is a limited resource we should exploit to the full. For this reason we see it also as an enemy: time, we say, is 'not on our side', we are haunted by the devouring, ravaging image of time which, like 'an ever rolling stream bears all its sons away'. Consequently we tend to see our lives, especially in a world dominated by material values, as a kind of one-way street down which we pass but once and hopefully ever-young. In this climate it is hardly surprising that old age is a fearful thing. 'I don't want to get older', said the actor Dudley Moore in a recent interview, 'I don't want my body to fall apart.' The visible processes of ageing are unwelcome reminders that there is little room for us in a society which has little to offer the old.

There are many ways of defining middle age but the best, because it applies to us all, is the time when it is first brought home to us that we are growing older. When we realize that our allotted span is probably half over and it is very often only when others draw attention to alterations in our appearance that we become aware we are growing older. This awareness, which may dawn upon us gradually or come as a sudden shock, is made all the more poignant by the stigma attached to 'middle-age spread', 'pot belly', 'brewer's goitre', 'spare tyre', flabby thighs, slack bottom, sagging, waffling, and wrinkling. Jokes about the ageing physique are nearly always negative, although traditionally those referring to women have had a sharper sting. From a loosely feminist perspective Shirley Conran recently rammed the message home to women and any middle-aged men who may happen to take up her book. Contrary to what we have been led to expect, she wrote in *Futures*, men can look pretty moth-eaten by the time they're thirty:

They start to go bald (and that can put on twenty years in two); they don't look after their skin so it looks as if someone has been cleaning the car with it for the last twenty years. Then the neck disappears in a fleshy roll and lots of them start to look five months pregnant. As far as losing their looks is concerned, men have as much to fear as women. In addition they have the male menopause or midlife crisis to worry about and this is 'neither a myth nor a joke'.

In one of her studies of a sample of middle aged men and women in America, Bernice Neugarten suggests 'that the central psychological task for middle age relates to the use of time, and the essential polarity is between time mastery and capitulation'. It is one of life's major ironies that at the same moment when we see time as a limited resource swiftly slipping from our grasp, we have never had so much of it at our disposal. The increase in life expectancy from fifty around the turn of the century to between sixty-five and seventy today means that more of us are living into middle age and beyond. Changes in the nature of work — especially the elimination of physically exhausting labour — coupled with better sanitation and nutrition have improved the general health of the population and extended the possibility of a more active middle age to groups other than the specially privileged. The reduction in the number of children in the family from about six in late Victorian times to just over two today has dramatically reduced the amount of time women must subject themselves to the rigours of the reproductive cycle and couples are now free to spend more time together during the middle years.

The emergence of the 'empty nest syndrome', when grown-up children have left home and the time and purchasing power of the middle-aged couple increases, can also be seen as having opened up a new market ripe for commercial exploitation. In the past commercial opportunism has responded to the knowledge that, at certain periods in the life cycle, people whose income was formerly tightly committed, suddenly have more money to spend; the creation of the teenager and the development of youth culture in the 1950s can of course be seen in this light. Similarly the

15

changes in the nature of the life course leading to the 'empty nest syndrome' as well as the wife's return to full-time employment, created the possibility of a new middle-aged market in the 1960s and 1970s and concomitant commercial interest in creating a new image for middle age. Michael Frayn in his novel *Towards the End of the Morning* has the financial whizz-kid Morris mulling over potentially lucrative ventures:

> Lots of markets still untapped. . . . Take the fifties age-group. Maximum earning power, children off their hands, ten years to go before retirement. Lots of money there, Bob. Sell them sports cars, jock-straps, buck-skin boots — young men's kit. They've got the money for it at that age.

From a more academic perspective Mark Abrams has pointed out that the period between the late forties and early sixties represents perhaps the most prosperous years for the married couple. These are also the years in which the problem of what to do with the additional free time begins to emerge.

In this new climate of sensitivity, experts and other commentators have accepted that the middle years have a special status in the life history of the individual precisely because it is during these decades that the physical signs of ageing are often detected for the first time. For example, Irene Friese, who is concerned with sex roles, writes:

> Theorists agree that there is a point in the life cycle when people experience a major transition into middle age (ages 44–47). As people age they become aware that they no longer look young,

may no longer feel attractive, and can no longer rely on their body to function unflaggingly. . . . The feeling that time is running out creates a psychological pressure to make the most of one's remaining good years; to seek out desired experiences before it is too late.

All these changes make it difficult for us to ignore the fact that we are being encouraged from a number of quarters to be aware of the physical signs of ageing and to dwell on their social and personal implications. Two of the most popular British TV series of recent years — 'The Fall and Rise of Reginald Perrin' and 'Telford's Change' — are both in their different ways concerned with their middle-aged protagonists' sensitivity to ageing.

Serialized for the first time in 1979 and repeated in 1980, 'Telford's Change' is about a highly successful banker who at 45 becomes dissatisfied with his intercontinental business and social life and attempts to opt out of the 'rat race' by taking a bank manager's job in Dover. Most of the tension in the story stems from his wife Sylvia's reluctance to abandon her London life and career, and the flattering attentions of one of her dashing male colleagues. The programmes attracted so much interest that immediately before the final episode Claire Rayner, the agony columnist, devoted almost an entire page of *The Sun* newspaper to the question 'Can the Telfords Change?'. Both the Telfords, she noted, had reached in middle age a crisis situation which had to be resolved:

They should be able to see where they went wrong — that he needs to communiate more with Sylvia, express his feelings for her more freely, and

17

she needs to demand more of him. Armed with that knowledge, they can talk, plan and build a new future for themselves that will satisfy them both.

The tragi-comedy of Reginald Perrin is the story of a man who at forty-six throws up his job with Sunshine Desserts and the tedious comforts of his suburban home to pursue several different identities and experiment with alternative ways of life. The success of the series owed much to the actor Leonard Rossiter who observed in an interview in 1978 that 'Perrin obviously strikes a chord with a great many people'. But the saddest of the many letters he received about the part came from a man who couldn't understand why the whole thing was meant to be funny. As we shall see, there is abundant evidence that increasing numbers of men and women in Britain and the United States are now taking middle age very seriously indeed.

2

The Menopause

For many women one of the most crucial events in middle age is, of course, the menopause. In a centre-page spread in September 1978, Diana Dors, 46, told *Sun* readers the change of life gave her little cause for concern:

I haven't reached it yet, but I don't think it's going to be bad. I've heard there are fantastic pills and things. I should exercise and diet but I don't. I just eat. I love food, so what the hell! You're only here once; so why not enjoy it?

Five years before, *The News of the World* had asked in 'The Secret of Eve' how old the smiling, well-dressed and youthful woman in the photograph looked — 'late thirties? fortyish? a well-preserved fifty?'. She was in fact sixty-year-old Eve Graham, Max Factor's chief make-up artist. How did she do it?

The answer seems to be a combination of common-sense, care, plus Hormone Replacement Therapy. HRT as it's called, began for her when her doctor put her on the Pill as the menopause started. The menopause just gave up and went away. Common-sense has kept her at 36—24—36, just right for 5 ft 4 in. She eats sensibly.

HRT became popular after an American doctor Robert Wilson published the best-selling *Feminine Forever* in the mid 1960s. In it he defined the menopause as a deficiency disease and claimed that some twenty-six different symptoms could be averted through oestrogen replacement:

> *Menopause is completely preventable!* No woman need suffer menopause or any of its symptoms if she receives preventative treatment *before* the onset of menopause. Menopause is curable. Under proper medical treatment, nearly all its symptoms cease in the vast majority of cases.

In those early days oestrogen replacement therapy was given considerable publicity in the United States through drug company promotion campaigns and feature articles in magazines and newspapers. A massive growth in sales followed and five million prescriptions for oestrogen were sold in 1975, despite the fact that only one and a half million women were in the menopausal years. In Britain a similar campaign to promote the benefits of HRT took off in the mid-1970s though it met with a more cautious response on the part of National Health Service doctors. A caution which would seem to be justified in view of the anxiety over the risks of endometrial cancer, heart problems and gall bladder disease. There are also doubts about the logic behind the treatment which equates the natural decline of oestrogen with disease.

Despite these reservations, large numbers of women are demanding HRT and one important reason can be found in the popular label 'the youth' or 'happiness pill'. The present-day rejection of ageing can only serve to heighten the level of anxiety surrounding the menopause. A letter began in *The Daily Mirror*:

> Dear Marje, I am 48 and have always had a wonderful sex life with my husband. I was also able to reach a climax easily, but suddenly I can't any more. In fact, I've simply stopped getting any pleasure from lovemaking. It's almost as if something inside me has been switched off. . . . I can only think I must have started the change and it seems as if I've nothing to look forward to.

Proops agreed the change can mean a sexual switch-off, 'An enormous number of women, from their early forties onwards, go off sex. It's a recognised menopausal symptom' but went on to point out her correspondent's sex life could be revived by treatment from her doctor, or by trying out new sexual techniques, or even reading a sex book or two.

Under the headline 'Why Doreen Must Stop Thinking She's Past It' Unity Hall quoted another letter:

> My husband and I have been married for 25 years. . . . I suppose we've settled down to being a cosy couple. He even calls me Mum which I don't like too much. And recently we've changed our double bed for two singles as we find we sleep better that way. Our sex life has been more or less non-existent since I started the change of life a year ago. My husband says this doesn't worry him as 'we're too old for all that'. He's just 50.

Unity Hall replied that the attitude 'we're all past it now' is very dangerous to marriage. Many women who have previously never been very interested in sex believe being older and the change of life are excuses to end their sex life. But they don't realize what a gamble they are taking with their marriage and should try to be more sexually exciting for their man.

Stimulation need not be solely for the man's benefit; post-menopausal freedom from risk of pregnancy and menstrual discomfort should make sex more enjoyable for the woman. According to Shirley Conran's *Futures*:

> Women who continue to have a good and active sex life can: Age more slowly. Look better. Live longer. Show least physical evidence of the change. Enjoy sex more.

There is, she urges, no such thing as being too old for sex; 'Use it or lose it' should be the new feminine slogan. Women should be prepared to make an effort and work at their sex lives and self-image is an important element of sexual identity — so looking good can play a crucial role. A 15 pounds overweight woman who makes the effort and slims will find 'not only are you less embarrassed when cavorting naked, and stop turning the light off, but you actually feel more agile, energetic and sexier'.

This changing attitude towards the menopause is epitomized in Claire Rayner's article 'The Bolder Older Woman', where the 40-plus woman is fast losing her image of being 'past it':

> We are slowly beginning to question the old wives' tales about the menopause. Not so long ago, many women believed that, during it, they could go off their heads, suffer melancholia, not just depression,

be stricken with hot flushes, loss of memory, become old and wrinkled almost overnight, losing all their femininity and sexual attractiveness and that they would lose all interest in sex themselves . . . but all the menopause does is alter her ability to reproduce. She does not automatically become dried up and useless simply because she is no longer a breeding machine. She can be — and a great many are — as sexually attractive as ever. Neither does the change of life cause a woman to lose her own interest in sex.

She goes on to question the myth that oestrogen, the female hormone, is solely responsible for making women feel sexy. In fact the position is more complex for it is the hormone androgen, which men too possess, which is responsible for the sex drive. Middle-aged women should naturally feel more sexy because after the menopause the androgen levels rise, following the decline of the natural antagonist, oestrogen.

This forthright hedonism contrasts not only with the traditional image of female sexual decline but also with the long-held belief that men have a stronger sex drive than women, a view which was until recently bolstered by academic and medical discussions of sexuality. Scully and Bart found in their study of twenty-seven gynaecology textbooks, written between 1943 and 1972, that they repeated traditional beliefs that the male sex drive is stronger than the female's, that women are frigid and do not enjoy intercourse, and that women are only interested in sex for procreation and not for pleasure. Others have also argued that the natural decline in male sexuality in the middle years, occurring at a time when a woman's sex drive is still strong, is frequently misinterpreted by the wife, who supposes her husband's lack of sexual interest is the result of her own loss of sexual attractiveness.

Accompanying the emergence of the bolder, older woman is a good deal of media publicity sanctioning relations between older women and younger men. As a woman gets older there are fewer men to chose from amongst her contemporaries. In 1961 there were 381 widows for every 100 widowers and by 1976, 425 per 100. In their study of divorce and marriage the Office of Population, Census and Surveys, published in June 1979, showed that in their second marriage 37 per cent of women marry younger men, and of these 6 per cent of women attract a man ten or more years younger. Once sex is accepted as not being primarily for the production of children but for the building of an exciting, loving relationship, and as a recreational activity, it becomes easier for society to disregard age differences which hitherto tended to attract censure and ridicule. Some commentators now believe a relationship between an older woman and a younger man is more exciting and even more 'natural'. 'Sex experts', wrote Liz Hodgkinson in *The Sun* 'say that the ideal combination in bed is a man of 19 and a woman of 35. That is when both are at their loving peak.' In January 1980 Rosalie Shann in *The News of the World* said she didn't find the news of Peter O'Toole's 45-year-old ex-wife marrying a young actor of 28 in the least strange. After all, Britt Ekland, Brigitte Bardot and Princess Margaret all prefer younger men. More prosaically, a 49-year-old housewife recently 'stunned her husband and wrecked a village' when she ran away with a 17-year-old boy. 'I know,' she said, 'our romance must seem incredible but to me it's a

24

beautiful, beautiful thing for us to have found each other.' The couple, who strongly deny the absurdity of the age gap, plan to marry as soon as the divorce comes through.

According to Shann this trend is partly the result of liberating scientific advances — specially hormone treatment which allows women to bypass the 'change' and not 'fall into the middle-age trough'. Youth-preserving beauty and fashion aids are another important influence on change taking place in women's attitude towards the middle years. By contrast men are still bogged down in the out-dated 'when-you're-past-forty-you've-had-it-syndrome', longing for retirement and allowing themselves to get fat and boring. Many of them even think they are too old for sex. This isn't, Shann says, what the modern woman in her forties wants so she may turn to a younger man who is more on her wave-length and mentally more in her age group.

All of which is a far cry from the world of the 'gigolo'. Whereas a man could legitimately purchase the affections of a younger woman by posing as a benefactor or 'sugar daddy', paying for the company of a younger man was seen as the ultimate humiliation for a woman. It is said that the folklore of Hollywood includes the question 'What are the four times in her life when a woman blushes?' 'Well, the first time, of course. Then, the first time with somebody besides her husband. And then the first time she does it for money!' The fourth time is when 'she has to pay for it herself'. In the 1930s George Raft was called a 'gigolo' because as a 'taxi dancer' in a dance palace he had been paid to dance with women. The taint of his former occupation lingered long after stardom. In an interview with a Hollywood fan magazine he had to vigorously deny he was a gigolo: 'One writer stated that I glorify the gigolo. Can you glorify a sewer rat? I know only disgust for such men; why should I exalt them?' Gigolos were an affront to masculinity; a man should provide for a woman, not the other way round. He vowed he had no preference for older women and didn't find them attractive: 'The majority of ladies who danced were middle-aged and homely; the sort of women who must pay. Few were good dancers, most were clumsy; many were fat.'

Today the term 'gigolo' has lost its pejorative overtones. In America the recent film *Gigolo* starring Richard Gere was a smash hit. The modern attitude to sex relations between older women and younger men is reflected in an interview with 48-year-old Sandy Fawkes, authoress of *In Praise of Younger Men*, who described her relationship with her 34-year-old boyfriend and urged other women to follow her example:

> Too many older women hide. They think because they are 40 they are past it. That's not true. You have a greater sex drive and a greater ability to give sexual satisfaction than when you are 20. Many older women could find great fulfilment in a younger men. Younger men are much more exciting and so much better in bed.

One advantage of a relationship with a younger man is that it provides a middle-aged woman with a partner who is not yet in the grip of the ageing process. TV personality Joan Bakewell, 44, married to actor—playwright Jack Emery, who is ten years younger, says: 'It's lovely, he keeps me young and lively. I find Jack very attractive. Men of my age are going bald, flabby and jowly, but he's not going grey and is very smooth.'

Soon after the 'Spend, Spend, Spend' pools winner Viv Nicholson, 41, was rushed into hospital suffering from a drug overdose (because she was 'frightened of getting old') she met and became engaged to 25-year-old Bernard Curran. 'I don't like older men', she announced:

> They are so subdued. I've always been attracted to younger men because they are more exciting. I like to be looked after by a man and I like to feel young. I do like to get my own way. So that may be another reason why younger men attract me.

This attraction is not one-sided: younger men apparently are finding the middle-aged 'mature' woman more desirable than the 'dolly bird'. In a national survey of men aged between 25 and 35 in January 1979, Joan Collins was voted Britain's top sex symbol. When asked about the secrets of her success, Joan told *News of the World* readers:

> A lady in her forties has more to offer than just pretty physical packaging. Trying to be sexy doesn't come from wearing a short skirt or letting your boobs hang out. It comes from inside.

Most men over forty, she said, find it difficult to match this sense of inner energy, they tend to get complacent and don't seem to care whether their hair is a mess or whether they have got pot bellies.

During the 1970s, then, a new stereotype of the energetic, attractive, sexy older woman emerged in sharp contrast to the more traditional maternal, asexual, grandma type. In a 1978 article entitled 'How Young You Look Gran', *Daily Mirror* readers were told 'The homely image of a wrinkled, grey-haired granny is as out of date as a penny-farthing.' Children apparently find it difficult to relate this traditional stereotype to their everyday experiences. Yet children's books and advertisements continue to portray grandmas in the old 'rosy, cosy, plump way'. More acceptable — presumably as much to the grannies as to the kids — is today's glamorous young gran image.

3

The Male Menopause

The notion of the menopause as an adventurous stage in the sex life of women is of recent origin; humorous references to older men who reject their matronly, menopausal wives to chase younger girls are an interesting indication of a long-standing double standard of ageing. The stereotype of the middle-aged woman as unfit for, or uninterested in, sex contrasts with the celebration of the sexiness of younger women in popular sexual humour. The turning of old wives into new has a long history. A seventeenth-century Dutch and German cartoon of 'The Mill for Grinding Old Wives into New' shows them being dumped into one end of a grinding mill and emerging rejuvenated from the other. A recent variant was the 1975 film *The Stepford Wives*, in which the men in a sleepy American suburban town have discovered a way of replacing their real wives with subservient robots which never age, never get fatigued by domestic chores, are tireless child minders and, above all, well groomed sex objects, whose conversation consists of endless mechanical praise and compliance. As the leading conspirator gleefully explains to the girl who has discovered this chilling operation, the robots are companions who completely fulfil the American housewife/mistress ideal. They also possess the additional advantage of being oblivious to their husbands' ageing bodies.

It has, therefore, long been accepted that a man's fancy would turn towards a younger woman when his partner's physical attractions fade — time-honoured behaviour sometimes described as 'the Aphrodite complex'. This double standard may have been more tolerable for women who accepted the belief that the menopause resulted in a — perhaps welcome — reduction or cessation of sexual activity and end of 'female troubles', but the publicity given to the sexually active woman and the call for equal sexual rights on the part of the women's movement has made the double standard less secure in recent years. Yet it persists to the extent that the actions of older men in seeking a younger partner are still regarded as more excusable than those of an older woman:

> I am 47 and have a good, loving husband and two smashing teenage daughters. Yet a shameful thing is happening to me. I find myself very attracted to young men. When my girls bring home their boy friends, I have all sorts of squalid sex fantasies about them and often can hardly keep my hands off them.

The writer of this letter goes on to ask for help to 'forget all this nonsense'. Marje Proops replied that women in middle age often have feelings for younger men, but most push such thoughts to the back of their minds by doing the spring cleaning. The guilt of this letter writer, who uses words like 'shameful' and 'nonsense' to describe her feelings, stands in sharp contrast to another woman's matter-of-fact acceptance of her middle-aged husband's interest in his daughter-in-law, even kissing her when they leave although he doesn't usually do that sort of thing. The daughter-in-law had said he had even asked her to go to bed with him. Unity Hall advised against making a scene to get at the truth:

> The thing to do is absolutely nothing, and the only words of consolation I can offer are that this is honestly not such an unusual situation as you'd think. My correspondent is right in thinking her husband would laugh at her if she confronted him with an accusation. He thinks he's only playing games.

Recently a new label, 'the male menopause', has been applied to middle-aged men who recklessly cast off a long-standing marriage. Some of those who have latched on to the term also use it as a catch-all for a longer list of problems which can beset middle-aged men and which often seem to be beyond their control: doubts, depression, mood swings, re-evaluation of self, attempts to recapture lost youth, and sexual problems such as impotence or the fear of it. Others prefer to use the term literally to mean that, like women, men have a hormonal 'change' and experience similar physical symptoms to those which are often associated with the menopause. Elia Kazan's novel *The Arrangement* provides a classic account of the self-destructive tendency of a successful advertising agency executive in California who seems to have everything made:

> Then something I couldn't control got into me. Men will know what I'm talking about; I mean that desperate thing that happens at forty-three which

31

I was, or forty-five or seven or nine. Anyway, before I realized what was going on, it was a different dance to a different tune.

He gives up everything to pursue a young girl and in an attempt to understand what is happening to him, consults a friend who replies:

You're just going through a phase. . . . I've seen it, even went through it myself, although with me it was just a matter of a few days. Some people call it the male menopause, hot flushes and all the rest of it; we have them just like the girls — behave eccentrically, doubt everything, not able to get it up, all soft-on and self-doubt — I know all about it.

In her analysis of the cinema's treatment of the female role in popular films Molly Haskell refers to the idea that ageing is more devastating for women than men, yet 'as recent studies of "menopause" in men show', she adds, 'it can be just as convulsive' for a man. Certain film directors have added fuel to the myth by exaggerating the degree to which women are affected by age — always in the guise of sympathy — or by focusing on those kinds of women who dread ageing most. If the age of forty is traumatic for a woman it is, for different reasons, just as traumatic for a man. According to Haskell's analysis the films *Sunset Boulevard* and *All about Eve* are veiled expressions of the anxieties of their directors, Billy Wilder and Joseph Mankiewicz, who were respectively forty-four and forty-one when they made them.

Another writer, Nancy Mayer, has said the sexual problems of middle-aged men stem from the 'masculine mystique' — the value placed upon being a

32

winner in career, sport and even sex. The adherence to a sexual performance principle, where numbers of orgasms or conquests are taken as an important sign of masculinity, provides problems for men who are reluctant to acknowledge and adapt to their changing sexual capacity in middle age. The sexual prowess of the macho superstud is a powerful image within our culture. Under the headline 'The 48 Hours of Love' Hollywood sex symbol Burt Reynolds, 38, claimed he once made love to 54-year-old Dinah Shore for 48 hours, almost non-stop. 'All I did was roll off once in a while, gasp for air and start off again.' To Mayer it is hardly surprising that middle-aged men have problems when trying to cling to 'macho' standards.

At a time therefore when a man is possibly worry-ing about his sexual capacity, his middle-aged wife may be experiencing a revival of interest in sex. The emergence of the bolder older woman who 'puts in fifty per cent of the effort and is therefore entitled to fifty per cent of the fun', may be a daunting figure for middle-aged men and is a marked contrast to the image of a youthful golden girl who is less experienced, even perhaps less demanding, and more pliant than an older woman. In the 1970s men have been con-fronted with a much more open acknowledgement of female sexuality. Articles in newspapers and magazines refer to the frequency of sexual activity for men and women at each age band. New sexual norms and standards are being given publicity which may produce problems and a loss of confidence in some men. In a centre-page spread in *The Sun* entitled 'The Men Who Worry about Love' Claire Rayner remarks that when she started dealing with readers' problems in 1973 letters from women outnumbered those from men three to two, whereas in 1978 letters from men outnumbered those from women two to one. 'Most of the difficulties men experience involve sex. It eludes them. It does not satisfy them. It goes miserably wrong.' One of the letters she discusses relates specifically to the male menopause theme:

Basically we've got a good marriage. But now with the kids grown up and off our hands, when we should be living a much happier life, he's just gone off the rails. He's buying trendy clothes that make him look silly. He's ogling girls at parties. He's talking about getting a hair transplant, and he's a misery to live with. He's gone off sex as well. How can I bring him to his senses?

Rayner doubted the male menopause was a useful label but acknowledged that many men experience a crisis in mid-life when they look back to their youth and forward to old age. A man will try to tell himself he isn't old at forty-five and is still the young swinger he always was.

The 'Aphrodite complex' may have a romantic as well as physical appeal. The 'magic' of a golden girl may provide a romantic appeal stronger perhaps even than the sexual. To the middle-aged man the younger girl can represent the fulfilment of the dreams of his lost youth: he projects on to her the perfect, fulfilling, emotionally satisfying, complete relationship which through his commitment to the daily grind of career and family he has denied himself. The sense that time is running out — what Freud referred to as 'Torschlusspanik' or closing-door syndrome — brings home to middle-aged men all the experiences they denied themselves in youth. Some have referred to this time in a man's life as a 'second adolescence', a period of strong emotions when the man who has lived life according to a disciplined work ethic stops and asks whether it can ever bring what he wants and sometimes decides to follow his feelings and break with long-established routines.

Judith Kurland, in an article 'Promiscuity in Middle-Aged Men', refers to a case in which a man chasing after a young girl emphatically denied he could put an end to his behaviour. Love, he said, was his main concern. Although he still loved his wife and would always return to her, he felt he had to sow his wild oats. In another case, when a husband's affair with a young woman was discovered, he begged forgiveness from his wife and agreed to end the affair, but continued to see her. On being discovered, his reaction was ambivalent: he wanted to maintain his marriage at all costs, but 'At the same time he could not conceive of ending his affair and felt it was the only time in his life that he had tasted romance and magic.'

The themes of middle-aged angst, the male menopause and the pursuit of a youthful dream girl have been neatly combined in Blake Edwards's popular comedy film 10. Dudley Moore plays a successful songwriter/pianist living in Beverley Hills who expresses his disillusionment with his life at his 42nd birthday party — 'They said that life begins at forty but they lied.' Next morning, on his way back from the party he catches a glimpse of a young bride (Bo Derek) on her way to her wedding, becomes obsessed with her youthful beauty and tries to track her down. Leaving behind his steady girl friend (Julie Andrews) without a word of explanation he pursues his dream girl, now married and on her honeymoon in Mexico. He watches her sunbathing on the beach and day-dreams about lying beside her. After saving her husband from drowning he has dinner with her and while her husband recovers in hospital makes love to her. But love-making is equally disillusioning: her casual, matter-of-fact attitude towards sex shatters the romantic dream-image of her he has carried around.

'I thought you were special', he says. 'I am special to me', she replies. Meanwhile, back in California, a distraught Julie Andrews is reassured by Dudley Moore's songwriter partner that there is an explanation for his strange and thoughtless behaviour. 'Most men in their forties go through a male menopause, they act strange for a time but they come out of it.'

This film is just one of the latest instances of media publicity for the male menopause — publicity which has built up in the late 1970s to the extent that the term now shows signs of being well-established in the public mind. The original source seems to have been an article published by Martha Lear in *The New York Times Magazine* in January 1973, entitled 'Is there a male menopause?' which systematically examined the hormonal and socio-cultural basis of the concept. In Britain a key event was the television programme on the male menopause introduced by Michael Parkinson in 1975. A rash of newspaper and magazine articles followed, and letters from readers to agony columnists began to flow in from women as well as men. Very often they attributed their problems, or those of their spouses, to the male menopause. Thus, in March 1976, Marjorie Proops claimed to be getting:

More and more letters these days from middle-aged men who tell me how they fancy some young female at work, and they explain that it is ever since they started the menopause, bandying the word around like they know what it means.

The trend continues. A more recent example appeared in *The Sun*'s 'Liveliest Letters' page in January 1980:

They say men don't go through the menopause, but I am convinced they go through some kind of change of life. Last year, at 46, my husband suddenly started doing crazy things he had never done before. He took up hang-gliding — though he has always been scared of heights. He started body-building — though he has never lifted more than his daily pint. And he drove me and our daughters mad with his overdose of get-up-and-go. Not only could he not bear to waste a minute watching telly or reading a magazine, he didn't like to see us relax either.

The first and (to date) only British full-length book treatment of *The 'Male' Menopause*, was published by two journalists, Derek Bowskill and Anthea Linacre, in 1976. For starters they disclosed that the male menopause was a topic ripe for exploitation. Whilst taking the concept seriously they were fully conscious of the influence of the media in shaping men's perceptions:

There is no doubt in our minds that the attention the media and the press have given to the idea of the male menopause has contributed greatly to the individual and collective opinions on the subject. In fact, wherever we have mentioned our book, the first reaction . . . was that people were either suffering themselves or knew someone who was. The second reaction was to refer to an article or feature in a newspaper or magazine – or to mention the Parkinson television programme. The subject has mushroomed over the months and gained acceptance as a myth and as a reality, as a joke and as a deadly earnest conversation topic.

Bowskill and Linacre accurately describe the male menopause as both myth and reality, a concept sufficiently flexible to embrace all problems of middle-age men.

Although the experts may disagree about whether it happens or not and about what to call it, the terminology seems to speak for what men feel they experience. Friends, wives, doctors and agony columnists, as well as many others tell of hundreds of men who define their problem as the 'male' menopause. It may be careless thinking or loose language. It may be a cliché of the media or a myth of the collective male consciousness. It may be men's rebellion against the supposed liberation of women or it may be women's way of putting men down . . . but it does work. It is illuminating. It does cast a telling meaning over what happens to many men in their middle forties – and, most significantly and usefully, it does inform us all about what they *feel* is happening to them. . .

The male menopause, then, tends to be used as a catch-all category for the various problems men may have in middle age: disenchantment with life, depression, fear of declining sexual powers, panic at time running out, the urgent need to re-evaluate past life. Part of its popular appeal stems from the way in which the label seems to make the various symptoms more explicable. In one of the letters which followed the publication of Lear's article, a wife said if she had read about the symptoms of the male menopause when her husband was going through it in his mid-forties, she would not have turned to divorce. In effect, the male menopause label would have entitled her to relegate her husband to the sick role in which his behaviour would have been seen as outside his control.

4

The Mid-Life Crisis

Like the menopause on which it is modelled, the male version is defined as an unpleasant condition producing changes that cannot be intentionally avoided. As such it is a term better known than its counterpart, 'the mid-life crisis', even though the latter has been widely endorsed as a more accurate reflection of the changes individuals experience in middle-age. The 'male menopause' strikes an immediate chord with the public at large. The term may appeal to women after years of unsympathetic male response to the menopause: if men now realize they have to face their own menopause they may adopt a more positive and understanding attitude towards woman's problems. Another possible reason for its appeal relates to the male reaction to women's liberation discussed by Marje Proops:

> My friend . . . told me that her husband had been getting at her and saying that since she's always going on about her blasted menopause and hot flushes and backache, what about a bit of sympathy for his menopause. When she told him men didn't have the menopause, stupid, he said: 'If you women want equality — we men are entitled to enjoy our menopause too.'

At the same time in many newspapers and magazines there is a tendency to challenge and discredit the term and suggest that when men and women refer to the male menopause they really mean 'the mid-life crisis'. In November 1976, Claire Rayner published a letter in *The Sun* under the headline 'Men Have Problems Too'. 'Can you tell me', it ran, 'something about this newly discovered phenomenon, the male menopause? I ask because at the age of 39 I am involved in it.'

She replied there was no direct male physical counterpart to the menopause, but both sexes could experience disturbing emotional reactions to ageing and it was widely acknowledged that 'many men go through a sort of midlife crisis'.

This interchangeability of labels is found in discussion of problems experienced by women where the mid-life crisis is also increasingly used to refer to the problems they experience in the middle years as the following letter indicates:

I am 44, depressed, frantic at not having achieved any goals. Wonder if I should change everything from lifestyle to country, city, everything . . . I am in total paralysis of mind and body and spirit. . . . Everyone I know of my age is like this and they try, have tried, everything from divorce to group therapy, to hormones to Vitamin E. Is this what is meant by middle age crisis?

Here is a woman desperately searching for some explanation of her distressing experience. Others are attempting to cope with what is perhaps a vague sense of unease or what some authorities describe as the 'silent crisis'. To all such people the term 'mid-life

41

crisis' offers a convenient peg on which to hang a whole range of difficulties men and women encounter in their everyday lives as they grow older. There are signs that for some women the term 'mid-life crisis' is a more accurate reflection of the changing nature of women's life in middle age. This new term more effectively symbolizes the equality of experience and opportunity some feminists are seeking. Too often, they argue, a woman's life is looked at in terms of her reproductive role and the menopause and 'empty nest' thus become the major events of middle age. With changing patterns of marriage and employment the role of the menopause as the central event in middle age is being challenged. In her bestseller *Passages* Sheehy enthusiastically advocates a mid-life crisis for both women and men during the 'deadline decade', thirty-five to forty-five.

The term 'mid-life crisis' was coined by Elliot Jaques in 1965 in his influential article 'Death and the Mid-Life Crisis'. He discovered a watershed, around the ages 35–39, in the lives of 310 painters, poets, composers, writers and sculptors. Some like Goethe, Shakespeare and Beethoven went on to produce great works, but the creative capacity of others dried up forever. For Jaques the central feature of the mid-life phase was the personal realization of the inevitability of one's own death. This could lead to an urgent re-evaluation of one's past life, one's achievements, one's failures and one's unrealized ambitions. There is the strong feeling that effort must be redoubled if one is to achieve cherished goals in the time left. The alternative response is resigned acceptance of one's lot.

Jaques pioneering paper stimulated discussion of the mid-life crisis. The result has been a broadening and elaboration of his original thesis to relate it more immediately to the problems of everyday life. The tendency for middle age to be defined as a stage in life with its own particular set of problems and solutions has also been influenced by psychological theories of the life cycle. Freud held that the key to understanding adult personality was its formation in childhood, but Jung said personality development in fact took place throughout the complete life course. He emphasized the importance of the second half of life — essentially a time of personality change and growth in its own right. Individuals who had previously been concerned with material achievements now had to let go and set off on a spiritual journey to broaden out hitherto neglected aspects of their personality. Erik Erikson combined some of the insights of Freud and Jung to produce a theory of development throughout the life cycle. He outlined eight stages of life, each posing its own particular problems, possibilities of growth, and crises as the individual moves from childhood to old age. The sixth stage, which begins at forty, involves a crisis of generativity *v* stagnation: the individual has to become less self-centred, more concerned with establishing and guiding the next generation or face a prospect of stagnation.

The ideas of Erikson and Jung have been particularly influential on the work of Daniel Levinson, one of the foremost academic students of mid-life. In his book, written with others, *The Seasons of a Man's Life* he develops his theory of the life structure. As we grow up we pass through a number of developmental stages each lasting for six to eight years, and each one linked to the next by a three to five year transitional stage. One of these transitional stages through which all men will pass is between forty and forty-five — a mid-life crisis. Daniel Levinson's work has been extremely influential and translated for a wider market in Gail Sheehy's bestseller *Passages: Predictable Crises of Adult Life*, and Nancy Mayer's *The Male Mid-Life Crisis*.

Together with other popular treatments like Eda Le Shan's *The Wonderful Crisis of Middle Age* these books follow a self-help human potential approach to middle age. They aim at making us more conscious of the passage of time; of the need to stop and re-assess our own lives, in terms of the positive yet painful possibilities of growth which involve relinquishing old attitudes and relationships. They all advocate the positive value of a mid-life crisis. In Gail Sheehy's words:

> Somewhere between 35 and 45 if we let ourselves, most of us will have a full-out authenticity crisis. . . . There can therefore be a renaissance in our middle ages. . . . If there is one single thing we really have going for us in middle age, it is a more accurate awareness of time. And if we don't get ourselves too caught up in nostalgia for what is past, we can use this more acute perception to excellent advantage.

In current definitions, then, a key aspect of mid-life is this reassessment process which should follow from the realization that chronologically we are at the watershed of life. Arrival at a 'certain age' — thirty-five and over — sparks off a sense of urgency, making us aware we are on the downgrade. We have less time left than we have lived and the remaining years must be approached with an urgent sense of our priorities if we are to make the best use of what is left

44

to us. This idea stands in sharp contrast to the sense of resignation, obligation and duty which accompanied previous views of 'natural' ageing. It is of course a notion which faithfully reflects the value we set on youthful energy. In effect, middle age is now being given the licence formerly accorded only to adolescence.

One of the most influential researchers into social ageing in the United States, Bernice Neugarten, has also suggested that the central task facing the middle aged is the use of time, and the basic tension is between mastery and capitulation. Paradoxically, the middle aged now have more time and also less time than ever before. Less time than one has already lived yet more time because changes within the family liberate individuals from the demands of child-rearing and home management. In this context it is not surprising that one of the most frequently discussed aspects of middle age is the previously mentioned 'empty nest syndrome'. Research suggests that for most married couples the maturing of children and their departure from the home is a liberating experience giving couples who can expect many more years of life time to think about their lives and how the future will be filled. Jean Kinney, who coined the phrase 'living with zest in an empty nest' describes some of the benefits of the 'bonus years' after the kids have left home. First and foremost she ensures her 54-year-old husband looks after himself by making him follow a careful diet and swim every morning. He is encouraged to cut down on his drinking, smoking, and high calorie and cholesterol food: 'I enjoy my husband in every way. I'm perfectly normal and I want to keep him alive as long as possible.'

The empty nest may provide the chance for the wife to fulfil herself and enjoy her 'late bloom'. Research indicates that women who lead full lives tend to find the menopause less of a troublesome experience. One problem however is that whilst this *may* be a time of fulfilment and self-development for the middle-aged wife, the blossoming of her life may be perceived as a threat by a husband who sees his career drawing to a close and is perhaps withdrawing into self-doubt. The conflicting expectations of husbands and wives in this situation are described in the following letter from a woman doctor:

> The empty nest brings about a shift in the power structure of the couple. It may allow the woman greater freedom for the first time: to enter higher education, a career, and this at a time when the husband's prospects may be diminishing and he has to come to terms with the fact that he may never realise his ambitions.

On the basis of his research with a sample of men from four occupational groups, Daniel Levinson has argued that middle age is also a critical testing time for the individual's 'Dream'. In early adulthood a man must have a Dream and create an initial life structure in which it can be lived out. The Dream an individual chooses can vary a great deal. It may be to become a great artist, business tycoon, Nobel prize winner, sports superstar or, more mundanely, a respected member of the community or a good husband/father. Whether the Dream is shattered in his twenties, or his thirties are spent are spent in a last effort to realize it, by the time he reaches his early forties a man will have to ask what has happened to his Dream.

Levinson believes that a man must successfully negotiate this period of 'de-illusionment' if he is to make the transition to middle adulthood and not stagnate for the rest of his years. But although the majority of the novelists, biologists and executives he interviewed had 'realistic' career dreams, very few of the workers in his sample had an occupational Dream. Their Dreams remained geared to fantasies about exciting accomplishments and gradually dissolved into problems of survival. Even those workers who hoped to become their own boss in a small business had to eventually forego their Dream. In quite a different project, a study of American automobile workers, Chinoy asked his sample to compare their dreams with what they'd actually achieved, and found they overcame the discrepancy by suggesting their failure was only temporary and they would eventually become an entrepreneur or farmer. Eventually they had to recognise they were trapped and for them the American Dream of becoming one's own boss would never be realized.

Bernice Neugarten and Nancy Datan have also drawn attention to differences between the working-class and middle-class. Middle-class samples saw early adulthood (twenty to thirty) as a period of experimentation and looked forward to a middle age of progressive achievement and productivity, in other words, the 'prime of life'. On the other hand, working-class samples saw early adulthood as a period of inescapable responsibilities, to be followed by a period of middle-aged decline: becoming a 'has-been'. Thus the process of testing the dream against reality which for Levinson is central — 'de-illusionment' — comes earlier on this kind of evidence for working-class men. Kenn Rogers has drawn attention to the increase in accident rates, suicides and signs of premature ageing amongst poor whites, blacks, American Indians and inhabitants of the American urban ghettoes. For them the equivalent of a severe mid-life crisis which cannot be resolved comes early in their late twenties and early thirties. It has also been argued that blue-collar workers encounter problems in early middle age as a result of their wives' changing expectations of their role. Instead of the strong, silent undemonstrative 'real man', wives now show a preference for a different cultural image, the more tender and responsive male. Arthur Shostak, referring to cultural changes which have taken place since the war, says:

> Far fewer blue-collar women and children now believe the middle-aged 'real man' is reasonably a cold fish, a lousy lover, a crummy father, and a callous son. Instead several substantial cultural changes seem to have undermined the old role expectations, and written a new part for the 35 year old blue-collar 'walk-on' that he finds even more difficult to play.

Many middle-aged workers thus face a painful situation caught between the outmoded masculine tough-guy role and the more sensitive role of the 1970s:

> Where once he was free to be a moody, enigmatic and maleccentric 'cowboy', he is now expected to aspire otherwise. He is to strive for expressive, open, and genial affability with most; deep-coursing personal intimacy with some; and erotic artfulness with a very select few. To his dismay this goes far

48

beyond this old genial ability to bowl every Thursday with the boys.

It seems likely these changing cultural expectations will place further pressure on working-class and lower-class man, some of whom will experience crisis at the onset of middle age.

The unrealistic nature of many working-class men's dreams, coupled with the social and cultural conditions which tend to deny any possibility of realization, contrasts sharply with the archetypal dream of middle-class men, 'doing a Gauguin'. The quest for self-realization, authenticity and artistic self-expression combine in the myth of Gauguin's flight from a mundane marriage and routine job to paint masterpieces in a south sea island paradise. Popular legend ascribes the flowering of genius in Paul Gauguin to a dramatic act of God transforming a solid Parisian stockbroker at the age of thirty-five into an anguished artist in exile.

The myth however has more to do with Somerset Maugham's novel *The Moon and Sixpence* than the actual life of Gauguin. Alas, the reality of Gauguin's life did not match up to this romantic interpretation. His change of direction did not involve a total rejection of bourgeois life, but was an attempt to create a reputation and succeed in the conventional art world. Gauguin worked hard to create the image of the authentic, primitive artist in paradise so that his eventual return to France would be all the more triumphant. Yet the mythical version of his life has been adopted as a model of the major changes which lie behind the mid-life crisis: the awareness that time is running out, gives rise to a 'now or never' situation where our dreams must be actualized or abandoned.

The myth attributes these changes in Gauguin to the exact meridian age, thirty-five, but the attempt to see his life in terms of a crisis at the mid point in life obscures the major crisis he went through at fifty. With his exhibition of his Tahitian paintings rejected by French art critics, and having failed to adapt to the demands of the natural life, the depressed Gauguin completed his master-work 'Where do we come from? What are we? Where are we going?', and attempted suicide.

Nevertheless the concept of 'doing a Gauguin' has made a crucial contribution to the modern approach to the mid-life crisis, defined as a time of reassessment and preoccupation with self. At a phase in life when social changes have created more time for reflection, the emphasis on introspection and re-evaluation has enhanced our consciousness of the biological processes of ageing taking place within the body. At its most poignant then, the mid-life crisis entails a confrontation with death, the realization of our own mortality leading to the need to reassess career aspirations and achievements, past successes and earlier dreams. Changes within the family, the death of parents, children entering the adolescent 'problem phase' or leaving home, as well as changes in the balance of power between husband and wife, all contribute in varying degrees to the need for a life review.

In the literature of the mid-life crisis there are countless references to successful individuals who turn their backs on their achievements or, defining their success as meaningless, look round for a new direction. Less well documented are the every-day experiences of the prominent people the first half of whose life has been stable, orderly and unfulfilling. To these also, middle age may seem the 'now or never' time, when the desire to change or realize the Dream surfaces. Yet this is the time in life when the opportunities recede for the vast majority — especially so in an economic climate which increasingly offers the prospect of redundancy or early retirement. When all the pathways towards greater self-realization seem blocked, resignation becomes a realistic strategy. It is only a small minority, as case studies reveal, of the redundant who make it. The cases cited by popular writers on the mid-life crisis are usually of upper- or middle-class individuals who have enjoyed career success in the first part of life. The backbone of Gail Sheehy's book consists of interviews with members of America's pace-setter set. Her assumption that the values of this group will eventually percolate down to the lower regions of society is too glib. As Rogers has indicated, lower-class Americans do already have their own mid-life crises, or as one individual remarked, life for them is one permanent crisis. Yet their crises are often without hope and almost always end up in inarticulate defeat. They would gain little consolation from books like *Passages*, with its advocacy of a 'full-out authenticity crisis' and a pull-yourself-up-by-your-own-bootlaces brand of moralism.

Nevertheless the term 'mid-life crisis' does refer to something real. Closely akin to the 'male menopause', both have passed into popular usage and have been adopted by ordinary men and women in their attempt to understand and articulate the problems which they encounter in the middle years.

My husband started his 'male menopause' a couple of years ago. He is 48 now and all the signs of his

51

insecurity are present. He brushes his thinning hair forward, conceals the fact that he is a grandfather, has started playing squash, and goes jogging every morning. I keep catching him gazing in the mirror and it's really pathetic.

The problem here is her husband's unusual behaviour, his frantic attempt to keep fit, look attractive and stay young at a time when he should be settling into the grandfather role. Marje Proops advised the writer to let the fever run its course and encouraged her to be more mysterious, 'do something spectacular' about her appearance such as tinting or colouring her hair, or having a frizzy perm and perhaps even take up jogging. Here is another typical example:

My husband is just nudging the mid forties and he seems to be fed up with everything. He says he's fat and doesn't have the energy he used to have and that he's dissatisfied with his job and his wife. . . . Frankly, he's a pain in the neck to live with, and he seems to have the idea he's going through the male menopause.

The writer was advised by Unity Hall to have a 'cheer up dad' campaign and encourage him to a bit of self-indulgence: to buy some new clothes and start a health regime because 'anyone who feels fat and unattractive doesn't have to stay that way'. His wife should also look at *her* appearance — perhaps she's let herself go and her husband 'feels he's a middle-aged man stuck with an unattractive wife'?

Not too long ago couples like these would have probably followed the conventional wisdom and accepted that as they grew older they would naturally have less energy, develop 'middle-age spread' and become more set in their ways. This traditional image of middle age presented mid-life as a phase of resignation to bodily betrayal and decline. In the 1970s, media publicity has helped to push a new, more positive and youthful image of middle age into prominence: one which extols the benefits of body maintenance and care for appearance. This new image, the origins of which can be traced back at least to the 1920s, is helping to produce a social climate in which expectations of the middle years are changing, imperceptibly for some, yet with greater dramatic urgency for others.

5

Changing Images of Middle Age

In 1976 *The Sunday Times* published a photograph of Sid Kroft, a young good-looking man with dark curly hair, Zapata moustache, bare chest and confident smile. We have shown this picture to a number of men and women and the consensus puts his age between twenty-eight and thirty. Sid, a successful American TV producer and entrepreneur who lives in California, is actually fifty-two. He sees the secret of his youthful looks in a rigorous diet and regular exercise. For breakfast he has:

> A *hand peeled* orange (never cut citrus fruit with a knife — goodness is lost that way). I need a proper cereal breakfast, mixed *raw* nuts, sesame seeds and oats all freshly ground in my kitchen with a tablespoon of honey, real apple sauce, home made yoghurt and half a papaya.

Everything organically grown. He never drinks coffee, alcohol very rarely, and mostly drinks herb teas and mineral water. Sid Kroft represents the prototype of a new image of middle age: the Californian future which supposedly lies in wait for us all.

It is hard to find a sharper contrast to Sid than the middle-aged characters who appear in saucy seaside postcards. Here the men are balding, paunchy and have dangerously flushed faces whilst their women have pot bellies and protuberant backsides, which, when not bulging from bathing costumes, are badly corseted. The expanding 'beer belly' and middle-age spread are seen as the natural accompaniments of the 'mum' and 'dad' roles. In this traditional stereotype of middle age, physical appearance naturally deteriorates when youth is past and there is little evident concern for diet, weight, body image, or 'keeping fit'. Apart from the annual fortnight by the sea, excitement and the 'best years of life' are over: mum and dad are looking for a 'bit of peace and quiet', the home comforts of a settled life, the armchair in front of the fire, slippers, and the hot-water bottle. Growing old is seen as an inevitable process — 'fate — something which according to the norm, cannot be combated by energetic self-maintenance and attempts to 'stay', 'dress', 'look' or 'be' young. A strong element of resignation pervades phrases such as 'growing old gracefully', 'becoming set in your ways', and 'it's old age creeping on'.

In his pre-war essay on the art of the famous postcard illustrator Donald McGill, George Orwell stresses there are no pictures of good-looking people beyond their first youth, and in this popular art form we find two opposing types: the 'spooning' couple and the 'cat and dog' couple:

> Sex appeal vanishes at about the age of twenty-five. Well-preserved and good-looking people beyond their first youth are never represented. The amorous honeymooning couple reappear as the grim-visaged wife and shapeless, moustachioed, red-nosed husband, no intermediate stage being allowed for.

Arthur Calder-Marshall later commented that the poor 'accepted middle age earlier' because it was a choice between new things for themselves or the children. McGill was simply reflecting the hard facts of life.

Amongst the more advantaged classes, however, there was a growing awareness of the detrimental affects of the ageing process on the bodies of both women and men. From the 1850s onwards medical men were urging a select audience that 'natural' ageing was influenced by a combination of factors: diet, work, way of life, childbearing, and changing sexual appetite. In particular there was an attack on the notion that men and women should inevitably put on weight in middle age. The Victorians were, of course, noted for their preoccupation with health. They flocked to the seaside, dieted, took pills, sweated in Turkish baths and invented a multitude of athletic recreations. The constant threat of illness made people more conscious of their bodies. They were more anxious to know how their physiology worked and hoped to integrate advances in sanitation and medical science with their religious principles. The search was essentially a moral one, to discover the laws which would ensure health and keep premature decay at bay. In this the Victorians employed a conception of total health which united bodily and spiritual well-being: *mens sana in corpore sano*.

Excessive deposits of fat came to be seen as a pathological condition leading to specific treatable diseases. In a course of lectures, *Corpulence*, published in 1850, Thomas King Chambers described the anatomical characteristics of obesity as an increase in the volume and weight of tissues affected leading

56

to a vast increase in bulk which was 'the most serious deviation from the standard of health'. He cited:

> The enormous quantity of useless blood there must be in the capillaries of Mrs S.: her actual weight being twenty-eight stone eight pounds, she has, in addition to that which she ought to bear, fifteen stone of fat, all as full of blood as healthy adipose tissue should be. And this is not accompanied by any proportionate increase of strength in the heart, and other powers which are to circulate this blood.

Corpulence, he complained, was not taken seriously by his colleagues who for the most part treated it with unbecoming levity:

> It seems to have been viewed by all as more a matter of curiosity than of true practical importance, and cases collected rather to furnish amusement than to increase knowledge. We read in the Philosophical Transactions of horses' backs broken by corpulent individuals, of walls pulled down to allow exit to their coffins, of the number of men that carried them to the tomb, and such-like puerile details; but scarce a word of circumstances which, as physiologists or practitioners, we would wish to know. All description of the individuals, of their habits, their diseases, the causes of their death, is omitted; and even the stature, by which alone obesity can be judged, is not recorded.

In his *Manual of Diet in Health and Disease* King Chambers explained the theory of dietetics, then in its infancy, and gave detailed advice on the choice and preparation of food. Differing occupations, he stressed, required differently balanced diets. One which suited the commercial, literary or professional life was not appropriate to those who pursued the 'noxious trades' noted for their specific occupational diseases. In a chapter devoted to athletic training he disposed of the popular idea that athletic exercise was inimical to the 'finer emotions of pity and honour', and induced 'blindness to intellectual pleasures'. However, it was typical of the period that his interest was less with cosmetic aspects of dieting and more with detection, diagnosis, analysis, prevention and treatment of disease.

The view that corpulence was visible evidence of ill health, or at least an awful warning of the decline to come, gradually found acceptance in medical circles. The worst of it was, wrote William Harvey, that until corpulence was far advanced, 'persons rarely become objects of attention; many have even congratulated themselves on their comely appearance, not seeking advice or a remedy for that which they did not consider an evil.' Moreover, the tendency to become corpulent 'is usually most remarkable about the middle period of life, when it is apt to terminate in gout, or some still more formidable disease'.

Middle-aged men and women who had allowed their figures to spread were living testimony to the perils of complacency and over indulgence: a regiment of sufferers from a self-inflicted wound.

At a time when poverty and hard physical labour stripped the majority of working people of their health, 'comeliness' and, in a comparatively short space of time, their lives, it was inevitable that the majority of cases of clinically defined corpulence were observed, 'most frequently among those on whom fortune has smiled, whose incentives to physical exertion are in abeyance, while the inducements of the table are in excess'.

The prospect was awful enough but the good news was that there were remedies to hand. M.R.A. Caplin produced a gallant defence of corsetry. Since middle age was typically the time when the tissues relax and muscular fibres lose their elasticity, the time was ripe to assist nature with a 'judicious application' of another layer of muscles. Along with others with an interest in the expanding corsetry trade he was a fervent advocate of support for the bosom for in middle age 'there is in all women a tendency for these parts to give way' and, if unsupported, to become unsightly. Although the body had a natural tendency to accumulate fat in middle age 'giving the particular appearance which the French call embonpoint', adipose tissue could be controlled and flabbiness restrained.

Victorian women who had no taste for diet, and for whom vigorous outdoor exercise was in any case largely taboo, could therefore discipline excess flesh with whalebone concealed beneath voluminous clothing. Fortunately they were expected to curve and bulge; the medical interest in corpulence was a far cry from the fashionable obsession with boyish slimness which emerged at the close of World War I. Affluent women did not buy their clothes off the peg but employed their own dressmakers to fit them with garments which disguised or compensated for any defects of figure. Women were also expected to dress to suit their age: 'mutton dressed as lamb' continued to attract censure and ridicule. Artificial aids to beauty — ears of gutta-percha, fake bosoms and anterior bustles worn to accentuate the buttocks — were, like cosmetics, considered to be an 'imposition on the unsuspecting public' (especially a prospective husband) and a 'falsehood'. A woman could go too far in trying to conceal her age. The journalist Mary Philadelphia Merrifield wrote in 1854:

> We violate the laws of nature when we seek to repair the ravages of time on our complexion by paint, when we substitute fake hair for what age has thinned or blanched, or conceal the change by dyeing our own grey hair.

If middle age could be medically defined as 'that period which dates from the completion of the whole organic structure, and continues until the decline of the innate force and hence may be called the autumn of life' it need not be without its compensations. Her bosom and abdomen hygienically and respectably supported, the middle-aged woman could become the epitome of matronly beauty. Dr John V. Shoemaker offered the following advice in the 1908 edition of his popular manual *Health and Beauty*:

> Do not make the mistake of dressing younger than you are. Beauty of form and face is not reserved for maidenhood. Matronly beauty is also recognized by artists as being sometimes of the highest type, and even old age, short of decrepitude, may present a beauty of its own nobility and majesty of countenance, or in the expression of the serenity which befits the decline of life.

By 1914 the idea that corpulence in both middle aged women and men was a sign of avoidable premature ageing was thus well-established in Britain and the States. There were definite signs of body consciousness among the middle and upper classes who had the time and money to worry about their health. The ideal woman was 'mature and dignified' and the ideal man not beautiful but 'manly'. Unlike his female counterpart, he was positively encouraged to exercise vigorously in order to cultivate his physique. In the words of Dr John V. Shoemaker:

It is . . . only by accustoming himself, by easy degrees, to unwonted exercise that the citizen beyond middle age can derive the indubitable benefit to be found in exercise among the mountains. Not only, with due precaution, will his flabby muscles be made firm and strong, but his breathing power will be improved. Deep draughts of pure air are inhaled, the heart is invigorated, the action of the liver stimulated, and the blood purified. Appetite and digestion are improved, and nervous irritability subsides. The skin becomes clear and regains the bloom of health. The eyes become again lustrous from the potent rejuvenating influences at work. Dr Hermann Weber, of London, states that mountain exercise has a beneficial influence even on the hair, and that the greyness of many persons in hair and beard has been diminished by a mountain tour.

Once the modern recipe for a slimmed-down, healthy and attractive middle age — diet, exercise, and supportive wear — had been formulated, further variations were possible. Amongst the more notable landmarks are F.A. Hornibrook's highly acclaimed *The Culture of the Abdomen*, first published in 1924, and the companion volume, *Restoration Exercises for Women*, first published by his wife Ettie Rout in

61

1925. As Hornibrook's title suggests, his interest was in the male paunch or, as it used to be sometimes reverently described, 'the corporation'. Of this, however, he did not speak in respectful terms. A line drawing of a businessman wearing a tightly stretched waistcoat did not illustrate the virtues of solidity and worldly success but served to underscore a cautionary tale. Such a figure was not only unbecoming, it was dangerously unhealthy. He made use of the now commonplace 'before and after' approach to show the benefits of exercise and diet. Photographs of the middle-aged paunch bulging uncontrollably and unhealthily forward were compared unfavourably with the firm contours resulting from his regime. Many of the remedial exercises were demonstrated by the author himself, a spry balding figure with taut stomach muscles and hence supportive abdominal wall. For those men carrying a 'middle-aged spread', 'pot belly', or 'brewer's goitre', Hornibrook's book was an unsettling read.

Although it did not include unflattering photographs of middle-aged spread, and was simply illustrated with line drawings, Ettie Rout's book was published with the same intention of improving appearance and health and happiness. Her scheme of exercises was specially devised for women, to prevent the dropped chest, round shoulders, hollow back, pendulous breasts and protruding abdomen that a combination of unhealthy modern living and the slow evolution of the upright human species tended to induce. The principle behind both regimes was the same. The abdominal wall is boneless with a tendency to bulge outwards or sag forwards and collapse like the weakened wall of a heavily roofed house and this unfortunate disposition can be accentuated by bad diet, posture, neglect, lack of exercise and, in women, hastened along by child bearing. The results — stretching and dropping of the abdominal wall and 'general loss of shapeliness' — can be remedied by special exercises, and there is no absolute necessity for women 'to go to pieces' following childbirth providing they follow her advice. Ettie Rout's system of controlled health was based on prehistoric dances involving rhythmic rotation and undulation which varied intra-abdominal pressure and thus strengthened the abdominal muscles. These gyrations were recommended for several reasons: they were a natural treatment of constipation, that scourge of civilized countries, and gracefully removed the need to take opening medicines. Secondly, they were relaxing and induced a sense of well-being. Thirdly, they helped improve personal health, and fourthly, they contributed to race improvement and race immortality. In his preface Sir Arthur Keith wrote:

It is my belief that the health of the womanhood of England would be vastly raised towards the ideal, if what you teach could be brought home to the lady who lolls on her Chesterfield as well as to the washerwoman standing at her tub. The human body becomes deformed from over-work just as much as from laziness; and if you, by a miraculous propaganda, could bring home to woman, and man too, that most of us could be upright and supple at 55, if such exercises as you teach were practised daily, something would be accomplished you might be proud of.

The *Medical World* recommended the book as a

guide to middle-aged women who wished to keep fit, and the *British Journal of Physical Medicine* noted:

> The Hornibrooks have certainly done great service to the lay public, as well as to exponents of remedial exercises, in emphasising the absolute necessity for a sound pelvic basis of the body!

This husband and wife team offered simple, sensible and practical advice and their booklet spanned the inter-war years in several editions (a paperback version of *The Culture of the Abdomen* was published by Penguin in 1957, running out of print in 1965). They emphasized the dependence of good health and appearance in middle age on a strengthened system of natural bodily support and relegated corsetry to a minor league. If corsets were to be worn, wrote Mrs Hornibrook as Ettie Rout, they should be 'sufficient to take up the work of support when the muscles fail from fatigue; but not of a kind to hold the body tightly or prevent the muscles working naturally.' Brassières, she added, were 'necessary and desirable from the age of puberty to prevent the sagging and enlargement of the breasts and were beneficial when they assisted nature'.

For men disinclined to cultivate flagging muscles yet uneasily aware of their protruding bellies, various supportive belts were on the market:

> You will be completely comfortable as this amazing belt gently but persistently eliminates fat with every move! It gives you erect athletic carriage . . . supports abdominal walls . . . keeps digestive organs in place . . . and with loss of burdensome fat comes increased pep and greater endurance.

'Get Rid of That', urged another typical advert, showing an authoritative medical man pointing to the waistcoated paunch of his middle-aged client. The solution was 'Regent Figure Control': 'a perfectly tailored, light-as-a-feather rubberless belt' worn over the underwear to reduce 3 to 6 inches off the waist-line without undue compression or discomfort. The belt also removes the causes of indigestion, flatulence, acidity, constipation, 'brain fag' and 'strained heart'. The list of benefits is almost unlimited and the pro-mise: 'No diet, drugs or heart-straining exercise'. This garment automatically massages fat away as you breathe.

Another typical ad, showing a side view of an erect middle-aged gentleman with military moustache and haircut, slices through his trim waistline to reveal a 'Linia Belt', a kind of corset which tightens at the back. A coupon will bring back the book: *The Linia Method* from the London-based firm with shops in Birmingham, Bournemouth, Bristol, Edinburgh, Glasgow, Hove, Leicester, Liverpool, Manchester, Nottingham and Southport. The manufacturers offered a Popular Model, a De Luxe Model, (in pure silk and extra light – if in Black 1 guinea extra) and the cheapest of all, a Standard Model. All prices included the Linia Jock Strap. 'You are', the ad announced, 'a "Bad Risk" with a wide waistline. Insurance statistics prove that the man with a large abdomen is the worst of "Bad Risks". The wider your waistline the shorter your life!' Don't neglect a sagging abdomen: 'The supporting action of the Linia Belt replaces dangerously displaced organs. It massages the abdomen, drives away fat, stimulates circulation, tones and strengthens muscles.' It also: 'restores abdominal health and gives youthful fitness as well as a youthful appearance'.

Despite exaggerated claims to control almost every disease known to man, eliminate the need for exercise, and enhance life chances, these belts and corsets were almost entirely cosmetic. The Hornibrooks were not alone in their view that a healthy and attractive middle age was only attainable through discipline and moderation. In 1925 Dr Leonard Williams's *Middle Age and Old Age* warned readers of the perils of over-indulgence. Rejecting the 'short life and a merry one' approach which tended to saturate the body with toxins, he recommended the conservation of health through judicious diet and exercise. The bad news was the first outward signs of ageing, which began in middle life:

As matters stand at present, the ordinary man begins to 'rot' at 30 years of age. The physical signs are not difficult of detection. They are writ large on the abdominal contour of the all-too-numerous victims. It is regarded as natural and physiological for a person to have received a considerable gain in weight by the time he reaches 40, and even insurance companies, which are necessarily severely materialistic, consider a gain of a stone between 25 and 50 to be perfectly normal.

But for those who followed his advice, middle age would not be a state of rapid decline: 'I plead for a longer plateau and a more gradual slope.'

During the 1920s and 1930s the interest in the connections between graceful ageing, health and beauty increased by leaps and bounds and helped to redefine middle age as potentially a period of heightened expectations. The notion of 'resigned middle age' found less and less favour. In his preface to the 1922 edition of *Old Age Deferred*, Dr Arnold Lorand agreed it was not yet possible to create a young man out of an old one:

> It is quite within the bounds of possibility, as we shall endeavour to demonstrate herein, to prolong our term of youthfulness by ten or twenty years. In other words we need no longer grow old at forty or fifty. . . . All this can be brought about by the observance of certain hygienic measures, and by improving the functions of a certain few of the glandular structures in our body.

Thus the signs of ageing in face and physique were now being seen as visible evidence of an unwise and socially unacceptable way of life which brought unfortunate cosmetic consequences. The new ideal was a youthful appearance, and the means were increasingly available to help maintain this well into the middle years.

From small beginnings in the nineteenth century the redefinition of middle age, limited for the most part to medical and socially advantaged circles, reached a much wider audience when the taboo against the use of cosmetics was finally broken. In his prophetic essay, 'A Defence of Cosmetics', Max Beerbohm had argued in the 1890s their use was becoming more common and 'most women are not as young as they are painted'. Cosmetics were:

> Not going to be a mere prosaic remedy for age or plainness, but all ladies and girls will come to love them. . . . The season of the unsophisticated is gone by, and the young girl's final extinction

beneath the rising tide of cosmetics will leave no gap in life and will rob art of nothing.

Sun-tan make-up was used by 'countless gentlemen who walk about town in the time of its desertion from August to October, artificially bronzed, as though they were fresh from the moors or from the Solent. This I conceive is done for purely social reasons.'

And a few years later a correspondent to *Woman* pointed out:

Many business women are forced to make-up because nobody wants elderly-looking people about them in modern times. They simply dare not grow old if they want to retain their situation.

Whilst by 1910 the editor of *Queen* laboured under the illusion the middle-aged woman had vanished from the face of the earth:

The disappearance of the middle aged woman is a marked sign of the period. Our London world is divided into girls, young married women, and old ladies in the 70s and 80s. . . . The 'fair, fat and forty' has ceased to exist. Women of 50 and 60 hunt, shoot, dance, play golf, and hockey, and drive their own motors . . . are forever on the go over to Paris to fit a frock or make trips on their own to New York, India, etc. Eternal Youth has come to stay.

6

The Hollywood Ideal

For the great majority the real cosmetic break-through was not to come until the Great War was over and Hollywood, with its commercial interests in health, fitness and beauty began to dominate the world of mass communications.

Because the Hollywood cinema was first and foremost concerned with the world of appearances — and, in particular, appearances that made money — it brought home to a mass audience the value of 'looking good' and ageing slowly. The Great War had hastened the collapse of the old order, and a new society in which the accent was on youth, rather than age and maturity, came into being. Business leaders needed an ever-increasing army of consumers of the goods their rapidly developing technology could produce and set about cultivating new spending habits in a wider public. Traditional values had to be broken down and puritan notions of thrift and moderation had to be discredited to make way for the new consumer values. Advertising played a crucial role in this process; it sought to make individuals self-conscious — more aware of their bodies and appearance. Advertisements conveyed the message that the image the individual had of himself depended more and more on the opinions and attitudes of others, which were in turn strongly influenced by his physical appearance.

In Hollywood the centre of this vast cosmetic enterprise was the star system. Rigorously disciplined by the major studios, film stars were carefully packaged for audience consumption. Whilst studio press agents bombarded the public with make-believe biographies, the beauty machine moulded faces and bodies to conform to ideals of physical perfection. New kinds of make-up including lip gloss, body make-up, skin freshener, hair spray, hair dye and setting lotions were developed and new techniques for disguising or removing blemishes such as toupées, electrolysis, and cosmetic surgery were created. And cheaper versions of these techniques were passed on to fans world wide. Mary Pickford (ultimately to branch out into the cosmetic industry) subjected herself to a rigorous regime, described in 1920 as follows:

15 minutes bending and stretching;
a cold shower (imparting a pink glow to the skin);
½ glass of hot water — and every ½ hour during day (keeps the stomach in good condition);
fruit or fruit juice for breakfast and one poached egg and dry toast;
if the weather was good walked to the studio;
had a light luncheon with no sweets;
and at the end of a working day took a hot bath, had an alcohol rub and 20 minutes lie down with a cloth soaked in ice water and witch hazel over the eyes.

Major maintenance came just before bedtime. Somedays her face would remain covered with make-up, clogging the pores, and so every night she began by washing her face well with physicians' and surgeons' soap and rinsing first with warm water, then cold. Next she rubbed in cold cream and wiped it off, repeating until the towel came away spotless. Then she proceeded, as she put it, to iron her face — rubbing a large piece of ice against her throat and face, pressing hard, stroking upward, continuing until the skin was almost crimson. If her hands showed any signs of chapping, she rubbed in a generous dab of camphor and mutton tallow. If she had been exposed to the sun during the day, she patted on buttermilk to keep her skin white! She would then carefully shampoo her famous golden curls. 'This is hard work,' Mary admitted, 'but it pays.'

In 1927 Lynn Fontaine addressed the women of America through the pages of the *Ladies' Home Journal* thus:

In sending out this bulletin to American women, I want first of all to ask you to make-up your faces. Study make-up. Put on your faces frankly, boldly — but with artistry. Don't mind what your husbands say. Let them object as loudly as they please. . . . They'll get used to make-up after a while, just as they are getting used to short hair. Not only getting used to it, but admiring it and being proud of their wives for being in the know. Short hair not only calls attention to the beautiful shape of one's ear, it is chic, which is another way of saying it is a symbol of youth, of the desire to be charming and attractive and of this day and age. . . . Long hair is dangerously on the edge of frumpishness.

71

Youth was most definitely 'on the prow'. The Edwardian taste for mature statuesque women had been usurped by a youthful style which those with totally unsuitable faces and figures often felt compelled to emulate. In December 1926, *The Queen* magazine described the question of suitable coiffures for elderly women as 'something of a problem these days'. Many had found a solution in the universal shingle 'with an unexpected and somewhat surprising measure of success'. But the writer warned:

> For a middle-aged or elderly woman to fall a victim to the shingle merely and solely because it is the fashion and suits her daughter and their friends is a mistake and often a fatal one. The younger women today are so well groomed, heads are so sleek, hair waves so becomingly set, that the older women should certainly be on their mettle not to look less well turned out, not to have that unkempt appearance about the coiffure which, in hair that has lost or is losing its colour, is so woefully unbecoming and also so ageing in appearance.

The desire to follow fashion was no longer restricted to the relatively well-to-do. During World War I many ordinary women had done men's work, received higher wages, and developed a taste for better clothing and cosmetics. The cinema helped maintain momentum. In autumn 1933, the writer J.B. Priestley had taken tea in a rural café in Lincolnshire, near tables occupied by girls who had carefully modelled their appearances on favourite film stars:

> Even twenty years ago girls of this kind would have looked quite different even from girls in the nearest large town; they would have had an unmistakable

small town or rustic air; but now they are almost undistinguishable from girls in a dozen different capitals, for they all have the same models, from Hollywood.

However, it was only the girls who had cultivated a cosmopolitan appearance; the young men, Priestley observed, 'looked their honest, broad, red-faced, East Anglian selves'.

Whilst it was mainly women who were the targets for the youth-orientated cosmetic and fashion industries of the early Hollywood era, male portliness, as we have seen, was not without its critics and, although masculine clothing and style did not change as dramatically as women's fashion during this period, the increasing emphasis on athleticism did not leave men unscathed. The career of the first cinema 'superstar' to have an international following, Douglas Fairbanks, neatly illustrates the trend. Fairbanks's many highly successful films were noted for the high athletic skill he exhibited in his role as the superbly fit, roguish and carefree male. He came to epitomize the ideal American and was for most of his life in excellent shape and, like many who depend on their bodies for status and success, he dreaded illness and old age. 'When a man finds himself sliding down hill he should do everything to reach bottom in a hurry and pass out of the picture.' Thus driven, he continued vigorous exercise and acrobatics until his death of a heart attack at the age of 56, knowing perhaps there was no other alternative open to him.

Hollywood cinema was a new, brash and youthful industry, carrying all before it. At the outbreak of World War II it was only thirty years old and its personnel, wrote Leo Rosten:

Are young — not so young as the public seems to think, or as the publicity would have it, but compared with other industries or professional groups, Hollywood would probably show a marked youthfulness.

His analysis of 707 personnel, including famous actors and actresses, revealed 46·2 per cent were under forty, and a third were between thirty and forty years old. On average actors were slightly older than actresses but his most important point was that the popular impression of the youthfulness of Hollywood was the product of selective publicity:

The numerous middle-aged or elderly 'character' actors in Hollywood are generally ignored. The romantic roles around which most movies are built put youthful actors at a premium . . . and gives them constant prominence in the public mind.

The prevailing public image of Hollywood was, therefore, of a place where ageing was less obtrusive than in the world beyond the studio walls. Films tended to ignore the problems of ageing and there were few attractive roles for actresses who were older, stouter or plainer than the stereotyped ideal. When Norma Talmadge, who was neither stout, old or plain was required to pass from youth to old age for *Secrets* (1925) one reviewer commented:

Miss Talmadge sacrifices beauty and youth to appear as the aged wife and mother. . . . But when she is a wee bit past 40, Miss Talmadge appears to have been reluctant to do anything more than submit to grey hair. There are no signs of sunken eyes

74

or thinnish neck, nor wrinkled forehead, or lines of laughter. She is 40! A beautiful woman with hair tinged with signs of age.

It is not surprising that no one wanted to play senior citizens; the genuinely aged, particularly if they were women, were considered fair game for ridicule. In this youth-orientated world they were scarcely the ideal sponsors of merchandise the cosmetic and fashion industries required. The star's job (both male and female) was to embody and convey to the general public the dream world they advertised.

Although a fantasy world far removed from the reality of the everyday lives of the majority of cinema goers, Hollywood made an enormous contribution to the redefinition of middle age. It took over the ideals of health and beauty established by members of the medical profession and united them with the lives of the stars. Beauty was not simply a matter of knowing how to wear the right clothes and make-up, it had to be worked at. 'When health is of such great importance', said Jean Harlow, 'movie stars can't afford to burn the candle at both ends. . . . I love the sun. I'd always rather walk than ride.'

Gymnasia, swimming pools and all the paraphernalia of the 'keep fit' movement were therefore part of the star's publicized stock in trade. Douglas Fairbanks was far from being the only athlete in town. Harold Lloyd's mansion was equipped with a swimming pool, tennis court, handball court and golf course where he trained intensively for each of his pictures as 'the glasses character'. Cosmetics and cosmetic surgery undoubtedly could improve one's facial appearance and mask the signs of ageing, but the true image of youthfulness was incomplete without regular exercise and a sensible diet.

Both these trends were cleverly capitalized on by that highly successful entrepreneur, Helena Rubinstein, who amassed a fortune of 500 million dollars. The Rubinstein beauty empire was built on her enthusiastic advocacy of beauty for the masses. She reassured countless women in *The Art of Feminine Beauty* that there was nothing frivolous or vain in wanting to hold on to youth:

> To preserve one's beauty is to preserve health and to prolong life. Through their determination to achieve these ends, women are helping to develop higher health standards. These standards are implanted in the newer generations. The fact that the children of healthy, attractive mothers have a stronger hold on life scarcely needs to be demonstrated. The beauty-loving, beauty-seeking woman — especially if she happens to be a mother — is thus making an important contribution to the building up of a finer race.

Gazing into her crystal ball, she predicted that the times when the woman of fifty would easily pass for thirty were not far away. A shift in life chances was taking place which would leave the woman of seventy free to enjoy a vigorous maturity:

> A woman's beauty will be a gracious curve from early youth to, shall we say, later youth; for the weight of years seems to be resting ever more lightly on women's shoulders.

The Rubinstein version of the image of middle age

as an extended plateau was accessible to all women who hearkened to her call. The cosmetics industry had democratized youth and beauty. To be sure women's bodies varied in height, weight and the relative proportions of their charms, and certainly not all women were equally good looking, but none of these awkward facts need stand in the way of a woman making the most of herself. It was important for women to make an effort to take advantage of the wisdom and the products hitherto unavailable:

An important part is always played by the desire to be lovely and the willingness to make small daily sacrifices to achieve it. If you follow the rules for your particular type or age you will keep your loveliness to the end of your days. You may not inspire a 'grande passion' at the age of eighty, as Ninon de Lenclos is supposed to have done, but you will retain — just as that famous beauty did — your birthright of physical and spiritual graciousness.

Once awakened it was woman's duty to preserve her feminine charms and keep her face and figure under close surveillance:

I would have women collect mirrors for their homes, and surround themselves with them. Let them have, as their first toilet requisite, even if they have to make sacrifices to obtain it, a triple mirror for their dressing table. Then, as soon as possible, a full length triple mirror for the bedroom or dressing room. And by all means let them have mirrors in their bedroom, the more the merrier, and mirror panels in their hall and drawing room. Above all, let them have hand mirrors on their dressing table, on their bathroom shelf. And at least one magnifying mirror, which are now being made so charmingly, with slender handles and coloured enamel backs, or with gay leather coverings for travelling.

With the aid of mirrors she could monitor her entire body and thus could work towards all-round harmonious development. Daily exercise centred around the abdominal and trunk region, where women showed the greatest muscular weakness and tendency to pile up fat, was particularly effective. It was a complete discipline ultimately designed to keep the ravages of time at bay and to conserve youth and beauty deep into middle age.

Rubinstein and other cosmetic merchants purveyed a message of hope. They helped to make women in particular more conscious of their faces and figures and the changes which occurred naturally over the years and marketed the idea that the ageing process could be controlled and premature ageing need no longer be an inevitable prospect.

Undoubtedly the Hollywood connection helped produce general improvements in personal appearance. By the end of the 1930s the taboo against woman's use of 'a little dash of artificiality' to enhance her natural attributes had been broken. The armoury of cosmetics was enormous, including permanent waves, shampoos, rinses, facials, eyebrow plucking and dyes, manicures, lipsticks, rouge, cleansing creams, tissue creams, skin foods, muscle oils, and astringents. 'Wrinkola' banished wrinkles 'quickly and completely after 48 hours'. Everyone who desired to retain their 'charm of features' should write to an address in

Shaftesbury Avenue, London, for a book entitled *Removing the Landmarks of Time*. In the States, it was estimated that a single issue of a woman's magazine could advertise as many as sixty different brands of cosmetic. In Britain the growing number of such publications was closely geared to the marketing of consumer products. Initially there had been stubborn resistance from women's magazines when the editorials of the early 1920s came out strongly against the use of cosmetics, but by the end of the decade they had capitulated and were running feature articles on beauty aids. Cynthia White in her book *Women's Magazines* informs us that this change of heart closely paralleled the massive increase in advertising revenue from cosmetic companies.

Although poverty and malnutrition persisted, between 1918 and 1939 observers noted a marked change in the looks of women in the towns. 'The prematurely aged wife', wrote Graves and Hodge in their classic study of Britain between the wars, 'was coming to be the exception rather than the rule.' Rising standards of living conditions, of course, brought new conventions into social life. Observers noted increasing pressures on women who wished to maintain their place in the business world to use cosmetics. Beauty consultants might go out of their way to underwrite health-giving exercise but working women often felt they had less time to spend on natural care of the body and, like many others, used cosmetics as a short cut. Powders, lotions and dyes could not take the place of health but were increasingly necessary for an acceptable social appearance. It was therefore important for women to have faith in the cosmetics they were sold — to believe they would produce the necessary effect. One general manager of a prominent cosmetics company put the whole issue in a nutshell:

> We do not sell merchandise in the sense that it is sold by the toothpick manufacturer. We sell a service to women, we sell a belief in the efficacy of mysterious liquids and grains. Remove confidence from this, and the cleverest chemical amalgam, the most powerful advertising campaign, the best system of merchandising, becomes valueless.

As the 1930s progressed men, too, succumbed to the cosmetic lure. Their dress remained conservative and undue interest in personal appearance was still regarded as a sign of foppishness, effeminacy, and probably homosexuality, yet increasing numbers paid greater attention to their appearance. Preference for a lean, clean-shaven, manly/military face made it possible for the cosmetic manufacturers to invade that male inner sanctum, the barber's shop. A large proportion of the money spent in these shops went, of course, on shaving materials but before the outbreak of war there were indications of awakening male interest in facial treatments and even the new techniques of cosmetic surgery.

Advertisements for bodily hygiene also became more prominent — body odour and the newly discovered 'halitosis' had to be guarded against by men as well as women. A Gillette razor blade advertisement in 1930 emphasized the dangers of not shaving. Below a picture of a distraught wife it implored:

> Keep an eye on your wife. Possibly she's not as happy as she seems. Sometimes you may catch her

face. Is she worrying about you? After all, most wives are loyal and proud, and rather reluctant to speak up. This may be far from the fact — but there's a chance she's distressed because you aren't as careful about shaving as you were in times past.

But the impact of the trade in male cosmetics, salons, cosmetic surgery and fashion on the male image of middle age did not really make itself felt until the end of World War II. Commercial links between the established tradition of the manly outdoor sporting life, physical fitness, and athleticism, were then strengthened and more closely joined.

By contrast, body-consciousness had a more equal impact on men and women during the inter-war years. Generally speaking, the Victorians and Edwardians had hoped to keep the human body covered. Clothing was designed to conceal as much of the body as possible and sporting clothes, though designed for action, were only slightly less voluminous than everyday wear. Medical men, as we have seen, might urge the benefits of figure control but only as a public health measure and certainly not for purposes of stimulation and pleasure. The naked body was not usually regarded as a thing of beauty and a joy forever. Indeed respectable people tried to avoid catching sight of their bodies to such an extent that some even drew a veil over the mirror in the bathroom. It seems likely that many married couples never saw each other totally naked: sexual intercourse very often took place in the dark, and when it did not, it was commonly only the erotic zones which were exposed. Painters, stage artists and others whose interest in the body was less than clinical, were regarded with a mixture of envy and disapproval, and the trade in nude photographs was clandestine and 'dirty'. Essentially the body was a clothes-horse, a structure to be decked out according to the dictates of propriety.

The movement to expose the body which began before World War I accelerated rapidly in the early 1920s. The accent on youth, epitomized in the forms of the boyishly slim flapper and her consort, came as a direct challenge to traditional styles. There was a corresponding decrease in the percentage of men and women having a visibly middle-aged body.

The public place where the body — or quite a bit of it — could legitimately be exposed, of course, was the beach. The Victorians did not believe in the beneficial influence of the sun's rays on exposed flesh, and on the beach kept most of the body decently from view. In Paul Martin's famous photographs of 'spooning' on the sands at Yarmouth in the 1890s, over-dressed working-class youths and their girls lie chastely on the sands — some sleeping, some in casual embrace. All the men wear caps and hats and all areas of the anatomy except hands and faces are concealed. Bathing and swimming were permissible only in cumbersome bathing costume. 'Warner's Rustproof Summer Corset: A Necessity for Summer Wear', could even be worn in the sea to prevent the female figure escaping from its fashionable restraint. Once, however, the cult of sunbathing had taken hold, clothes were shed, beachwear cut down to cover the bare essentials, and sun-burned skin transformed from the stigma sign of lowly outdoor physical labour to the great status symbol of youth, fitness and beauty.

Belief in the health-giving rays of the sun first appeared on the Continent. In Germany in the 1890s sunshine clinics were opened for the treatment of the tubercular. Beauty consultants cautiously began to advise the public they need not shield themselves continuously from the sun. Readers of *Girls' Own Paper* were told not to be afraid of sunshine. It was a restorative and it didn't matter if it made you brown. Published in London in 1902, *The Art of Being Beautiful* pointed out that the rays of the sun were harmless if sampled in moderation. Open air life was not dangerous to those in delicate health but was the best means of acquiring 'a robustness that is of itself a large fraction of beauty'.

There were still many, however, who disapproved of sun bathing and the resultant darkening of the skin. Not surprisingly, one of the first film stars to make beach life acceptable was Douglas Fairbanks for whom sand, sea and sun created an ideal athletic arena. Going against the prevailing trend, he allowed his darkened face to appear in films and the popular press. Other celebrities soon followed suit.

In France the spread of sunbathing was linked with the development of the Riviera or Côte d'Azure where, from about 1920 onwards, rich and famous people began to stay during the summer. Previously it had been thought the hot summers were unhealthy and the privileged classes had flocked there only during the mild winters. For artists such as Aldous Huxley, Scott Fitzgerald, Somerset Maugham, Isadora Duncan and many others, exposing most of one's body on the beach proved more and more attractive. Within a short space of time the young and sophisticated had taken over the Riviera summer, leaving the winter to the old. Setting a trend many more lowlier resorts were to follow, new swimming pools were built and the beaches improved. For the first time for almost a century, the beach became one of the few places where the average human body could be freed from the confines of stuffy clothing and publicly displayed.

From that point the search for the sun rapidly developed into a major vacational task. The emergence of mass leisure transformed the suntan into a hallmark of a happy, healthy holiday — an unmistakable sign one had been away and unbuttoned at least into casual clothing. 'The skin of the average overclothed man is white, spotty and inelastio!', stated an American article of 1929, but 'the skin of a healthy man is brown, smooth and sleek.'

The seaside was no longer simply advertised as picture postcard world where kiddies went for donkey rides or adults strolled leisurely along the coast taking in the castles and lofty cliffs. Now the publicists' vision was of a place where scantily clad girls frolicked on the beaches and in the waves. A popular poster extolling the Côte d'Azure showed a bronzed, sylph-like girl standing on the shore extending her arms to an enormous sun radiating the message 'Le Soleil Toute l'Année'. In Britain the more homely resort of Bridlington was promoted by the LNER as one enormous beach crowded with lively young men and women absorbed in the joys of bathing, boating and beach sport.

In keeping with this new image many British seaside resorts began to monitor their hours of sunshine. Those who could not afford the increasingly popular holidays in the South of France could at least take a train to the 'Cornish Riviera', or Scarborough, or Blackpool where the sun, if you believed the publicity, always shone. The beaches and the new swimming pools were crowded. In America, wrote an observer in 1934:

During the last few summers each weekend there has been a great exodus of people to the country and the beaches. No matter what the fashion columns have to say about tan, whether it be unfashionable or not, a large section of the population, male and female, strive each summer to acquire the colour of a beach lifeguard, often with some risk to health, frequently not so robust as a lifeguard's.

When not actually shining, reminders of the sun rising and setting appeared on all manner of domestic objects: cigarette cases, suburban stained glass windows, garden gates, fireplaces, radios, and at British seaside resorts, in the ubiquitous saucy seaside postcard. The image of the sun was everywhere and had come to be loved as much for its cosmetic and decorative virtues as for any health-giving properties it might possess. 'I've got masses of lovely oil to rub all over myself', said Amanda in Noel Coward's *Private Lives*, 'When I'm done to a nice crisp brown you'll fall in love with me all over again.'

A glance at any collection of family snapshots taken in the 1920s and 1930s will show how popular sunbathing had become. The mass display of partially clothed flesh in all its variant forms is a clear reflection of changing attitudes towards the body. Isabella might write to *Woman's Magazine* in 1934 for advice about 'What to do about some of these very modern ideas like sunbathing in the garden in bathing costumes, which may be all very well but shocks her old servants, the village and many of her old friends' *and* be primly advised to give it up, but there were many who thought differently. Alongside the influence of the cinema, the cosmetic revolution, and the medical interest in health and efficiency, enthusiasm for sunbathing had a number of important long-term effects on attitudes towards ageing. Firstly, it legitimated public display of the body and, in so doing, brought together for the first time in history large numbers of people in relative states of undress. It thus became inevitable that individuals should compare the size, style and presentation of their bodies with the often less ideal, living flesh of their fellows. Originating in Hollywood the mass marketing of images of beautiful people with its emphasis on youth added spice and a new competitive element to the cosmetic quest for health, fitness and beauty.

In 1921 a new institution was born: the first Miss America Pageant on the beach at Atlantic City 'To develop a higher appreciation of the beautiful in young womanhood by the American public'. The winner, who was chosen from eight finalists, wore the traditional bathing costume revealing only her legs and knees but the occasion was an opportunity for the display of the new figure-hugging bathing suit. From this moment bathing costumes were synonymous with beauty contests. Years before, Bernarr McFadden, the successful and fanatical physical culturist, had shown the way when he visited Britain and organized a competition to single out the epitome of healthy young womanhood — and married the winner. Now the press took up the theme and popular newspapers began to print photographs of contestants clad only in the new bathing suits. *London Life* ran a Seaside Undress Wear Competition and featured pin-ups of bathing beauties, female athletes, and 'physiculturists'. By October 1939, the social climate was safe enough for *Tit-Bits* to print the picture of a wholesome smiling young girl in a two-piece bathing costume on its front cover.

'Excess fat' became the catch word of the day:

Are you beginning to show a slight thickening round the waistline which may turn into ugly 'middle-age spread'? Well, you can get rid of excess fat by drinking a daily glass of hot water with a little Limestone Phospate in it. This pleasant effervescing drink flushes out food waste, breaks down fatty tissue, tones up the system so that all fat-forming residue is regularly eliminated. Start taking Limestone Phosphate today.

Excess fat was the new menace to health and figure:

Pity the poor fat woman — the butt of many taunting jokes — never able to look chic and stunning in even the most expensive frocks. And too, excess fat is dangerous to health as Insurance Companies well know who refuse overweights.

Kruschen salts would help and the solution could be speeded up 'by going lighter on potatoes, pastries and fatty meats'. So great was the enthusiasm for losing weight that manufacturers were able to cash in on the inability of many people to stick religiously to a diet and advertisements for slimming laxatives, medicines, external creams, bath preparations, and special foods spread throughout the media.

Some of the drugs on sale were positively danger-ous. In the States, where food and drug lesiglation left much to be desired, the discovery that sodium dinitrophenol, a chemical with weight-reducing properties, was dangerous to health did not prevent its manufacture in tablet form. Advances in the science of nutrition helped to bring a healthier approach to problems of overweight. The better-off were changing to lighter meals of cereals, salads and fruit, and the discovery of calories and vitamins enhanced health consciousness, though health-food shops were still regarded by the conservative British as too close for comfort to the lunatic fringe.

Higher nutritional standards were closely linked with an interest in 'keeping fit'. The phrase 'keep fit' in the early nineteenth century meant 'keep-fit for military service'. In 1930s Britain, the keep-fit movement was closely geared to developments in Europe and the United States. The word 'hiking' was imported from America though the fashion was German: 'We have', wrote a camping club official in *The Daily Express*, '3,000 members. Most of these are solitary "hikers" who carry all their kit with them.'

Soon the railways and the clothing manufacturers would exploit the vogue and hikers with their unisex berets, open-necked shirts, shorts, and rucksacks would be encountered throughout the countryside. During the course of his *English Journey* J.B. Priestley came across groups of hikers and cyclists setting out across the hills and moors outside Bradford:

> Before we used to set out in twos and threes, in ordinary walking clothes for our Sunday Tramps. Now they were in gangs of either hikers or bikers, twenty or thirty of them together and all dressed for their respective parts. They almost looked German. We passed the hikers very early on our journey, and so I cannot say very much about them except to doubt whether this organized, semi-military, semi-athletic style of exploring the countryside is an improvement upon our old casual

rambling method. These youngsters look too much as if they were consciously taking exercise.

In November 1936 *The Times* suggested even more effort should be made to improve the nation's fitness. King Edward VIII was cited as an example of a truly fit man and a King George V memorial fund established for playing fields. Many women were persuaded to join the newly inaugurated Women's League of Health and Beauty. At the same time in Germany the Nazi 'Strength through Joy' campaign featured party rallies with mass callisthenics to celebrate Germanic corporal excellence, symbolizing the subordination of the disciplined body to a higher authority. A year later the film *Keep Fit* (theme song: 'Biceps, Muscle and Brawn') starred the popular comedian George Formby, as a seven stone weakling. And some time during this period the cartoonist Pont included his 'British Character' series in *Punch*. Included was the 'Importance of Exercise': a figure steadfastly walking round the deck of a ship in the teeth of a gale. Beneath it he drew two men facing each other: one athletic, with a muscular chest and huge biceps gazing in astonishment at the other, a bald man, in vest and shorts, looking down in disbelief at his huge paunch.

7

Looking Good and Feeling Great I:

Images invite comparisons. They are constant reminders of what we are, what we might have been, and what we might become. Riding high on the tide of youth, fitness and beauty, Hollywood presented endless images of a glamorized lifestyle in which the struggle against growing drab and old played a central part. In hot pursuit of sales, advertisers sought to make people more conscious of their appearance and aware that bodily imperfections need no longer be regarded as 'natural' and inevitable. If your body failed to live up to the ideal, a thousand and one products were available to remedy specific defects and to sustain the youthful energy necessary to carry on the struggle. Even 'Sun Maid Raisins' could keep you 'young at fifty'.

Inseparable from the whole process is, of course, sex. The movies helped break down the old taboos and to establish new sterotypes and norms. In C.B. de Mille's *Why Change Your Wife* (1920), Gloria Swanson reclaimed the husband her drab appearance had driven into the arms of another woman by buying new clothes and having a new hairdo. Glamour is sex appeal and the glamorization of life makes it difficult for us to imagine people who look old having any kind of sex life. In the pungent words of an overweight middle-aged office cleaner:

> The younger generation if they see any older person making a fuss of another or summat like that say: 'Oh look at the silly old fools.' Why are you silly for just showing a bit of affection for somebody, just because you are getting old?'

At the end of the last war, women who were worried about the way they had aged while their husbands were away in the armed forces were advised to prepare them in advance with humorous references to their greying hair and matronly figures. This rueful approach to the ravages of time is enshrined in the saucy seaside postcard and in a changing climate this attitude to ageing still persists. It can be found in films about British working-class life — *Saturday Night and Sunday Morning, The Family Way, Poor Cow* and in TV characters like Stan and Hilda Ogden in 'Coronation Street', Mr and Mrs Brandon in 'I Didn't Know You Cared', and Tony Garnett's documentary play for television, 'Hard Labour'.

It is much easier to associate middle-aged stars, like Bardot, whom one newspaper proclaimed was 'fabulous at forty', with sexuality. The gulf stretching between the world of the 'beautiful people' and everyday life is symbolically bridged by these celebrities whose onerous duty is to personify the triumph of youth over age. Joan Collins, star of *The Stud* and *The Bitch* makes no attempt to disguise the fact that she is middle aged but does admit she has to work hard to preserve her looks. After spending most of her life in the film industry she has become one of the most celebrated symbols of sexually dynamic middle age. What she calls her 'late blooming Renaissance', is a tribute to lots of exercise and a sparing diet. Brigitte Bardot also shows no signs of losing the glamorous image nurtured on natural foods, and sustained by walking, swimming, cycling, skiing and dedicated sun-bathing. Older than Bardot, or Collins, the English actress Moira Lister is still an international beauty — personal diet, jogging, yoga, and hard work have helped her to retain a figure she is not ashamed to display on stage in frank love scenes with a much younger man.

The public image of the middle-aged star, therefore, is of a life disciplined by dieting, cosmetics and all the varieties of exercise it is possible to imagine. The gymnastics of Douglas Fairbanks almost pale into insignificance. Roger Moore — 'You'd be surprised what he does to keep handsome' — pursues a rigorous daily regime of exercise and careful eating in order to stay in work:

> This week Roger Moore is 49, but he barely looks 40. . . . . In Roger's case not only have the few signs of maturity improved him, but his face appears to grow younger year by year. How does he manage it?

> The answer is that the strenuous parts he was first given in Hollywood led him to evolve a system of Swedish drill to keep toned up. At weekends his routine includes swimming and tennis. He weighs 12 stone, has given up cigarettes and is a careful drinker:

> Like fellow Fabergé director Cary Grant, he is rarely seen without something of a sun-tan. And

92

with his fiftieth birthday just a year ahead you'll still never see him enter a room without every female there turning to look. Just the way it's always been.

In the movie business 'there's no scope', said Paul Newman (54), 'for fat heroes'. In September 1979, *Woman's Own* drew attention to yet another middle-aged star, Sean Connery, vigorously absorbed 'Keeping fit for his next role as James Bond. It's tough work being a hero — you can't afford to wallow around getting flabby.' Others who are prepared to be interviewed, photographed or filmed during their work-outs include Clint Eastwood, Warren Beatty and singers Engelbert Humperdinck and Tom Jones. For them the rewards are threefold: firstly, a good appearance which has high commercial value; secondly, enhanced sex appeal; and thirdly, a sense of personal well-being. A sustained capacity for hard work and play keeps the physical and social disabilities associated with ageing at bay. Some, of course, are more dedicated than others. The comedian Charlie Drake is said to have taken up jogging after unkind remarks from fans about his spreading waistline:

I was getting fed-up with making love in the dark, so I took up running on the spot every morning and living on a small tin of red salmon and a tin of tangerines a day. I lost two stones in three months — and I feel great. In fact, I feel so virile I'm sure I'll be getting into trouble any day now. I started my exercise and health regime for purely sexual reasons and it has paid off.

This emphasis on cosmetic factors reflects idealized

standards of physical ageing. In fiercely competitive California, ageing is a sign of defeat. A slim, sun-tanned physique, and an unlined and smiling face, topped by luxuriant hair, symbolizes the unending struggle against physical decline only the spirit of energetic youthfulness can undertake. From Los Angeles, author and critic Clive James recently wrote:

> You can't be in town two days without feeling the urge to take better care of yourself, drink more orange juice, run five miles before breakfast, do something about that wilting bicep, live forever. It is but a short step to your first face-lift. Suddenly it seems a crime to be unhealthy.

Judged by these rigorous standards many of us are weighed in the balance and found wanting: the middle-aged population is visibly 'out of shape'.

The new image of middle age, therefore, incorporates a number of remedies for the ills the flesh is heir to. Nowadays there is no need to become over-weight, wrinkled, go grey, lose our hair, and suffer from waning energy and declining sexual powers – in other words, to be unfit. If we look after our bodies and adopt a positive attitude to ageing we will enjoy the benefits of youthfulness deep into the middle years. A rational conservationalist attitude towards our own bodies can prolong the desirable attributes of youth – flexibility, adaptability and an energetic outlook. Thus we can welcome the confidence and maturity of the mid-thirties, yet also feel we are still young looking, attractive and energetic – still able to engage in sport and sexual activity at near full capacity. The new ideal is to stay thirty-five for ever.

This updated vision of youth, fitness and beauty

has four main ingredients. Firstly, a pseudo-science of the body which reduces it to a machine to be tuned up, repaired and serviced (in health education pamphlets the middle-aged body is often compared to a run-down used car); secondly, various techniques for repairing damage and preventing further break-down; thirdly, the cultivation of an energetic lifestyle and, fourthly, a strong element of fashionable styliza-tion. Taken together these facets of the contemporary image of middle age encourage us to be increasingly preoccupied with our bodies and the image we present during the course of our every day lives. In this context the battle against ageing is not only a source of personal pleasure and profit; it becomes a social duty.

It is often argued that we in the Western world have developed a sedentary and unhealthy way of life considerably at odds with our evolutionary heritage. Our work no longer demands the physical exercise our bodies need and, to add insult to injury, we fill ourselves with calories which remain uncon-verted into energy and lie about us in the visible accretions we complacently accept as an inevitable part of middle age. It has been estimated that nearly half the British population is overweight and the middle aged comprise the fattest group. According to figures collected by the British Nutrition Founda-tion, in the age range 40–59, 79 per cent of working-class women are overweight, along with 57 per cent of middle-class women, and 49 per cent from the upper class. Large numbers of middle-aged men (not in general as fat as middle-aged women who have a greater tendency to accumulate deposites of sub-cutaneous fat) are also overweight. As far as the United States is concerned, two-thirds of the population over fifty are said to carry excess weight. Published for several decades, actuarial tables reveal an association between fatness, heart disease, blood pressure, diabetes, gall stones, painful knee joints and several other complaints. Heavy people do not make old bones.

Pressures to make us conform to medical averages of body size have been mounting for some time. According to one health education booklet:

> Whether they realise it or not, about half the people [in Britain] weigh more than is good for them. That means that there is a 50/50 chance you are a fatty. Don't argue. Let's just see how you shape up. Do you find it difficult to squeeze into some of your old clothes? That's fat. Try bobbing up and down naked in front of a full-length mirror. Does your flesh joggle like a jelly? That's fat. Pinch the skin at the back of your upper arm, half-way between shoulder and elbow. Is the fold of skin more than about an inch thick? That's very fat.

Because it is visible, fat is the easiest target for health propagandists. Recognition of the fact that fatness is not necessarily a defect — some of those, for example, who appear fat do have heavy muscles, and obesity is not always easy to define — has not impeded the agitation against overweight. Wide variations in actual body shapes and sizes provide an ideal market for remedial products for the middle aged. The common factor here is the equation 'keeping fit' = 'keeping in shape'. One enthusiastic exponent of health and fitness for the masses is comedian Roy Castle, active front man to the BBC's popular keep-fit TV series, 'Feeling Great'. According to Penny

Burton in *The Daily Mirror*'s 'Slimmers Club' column, he 'got millions of fans jumping and jogging along with his exercises' in the show, 'Feeling Great'. Four days later a reader wrote:

Roy Castle's 'Feeling Great' fitness programme on Sundays seems to be doing the trick. I'm judging by the number of people who come into the bookshop where I work asking for keep-fit books. The programme is making people keen to be fitter — and a good thing too.

Programmes of health education and preventive medicine aim to create a moral climate which excludes lifestyles dangerous to health and ultimately costly to the health service. As it becomes clearer that the degenerative diseases which tend to become evident during the middle years can be combated with exercise and diet, health educators are making greater efforts to bring this lesson to the attention of the public. Their problem is to persuade people to change their way of life. In effect a successful health education programme would completely re-orientate the routine lives of a large proportion of the population and one of the most effective weapons in the armoury has proved to be cosmetic: an explicit comparison of the disadvantages of an appearance of over-indulgence with images of exuberant fitness, social success, and well-being.

A key figure in the campaign, therefore, is 'The Slob'. The slob is the epitome of unfitness; slobs are people who eat too much, let themselves go and are careless about their appearance. They are casual, lack self-discipline and are far too relaxed and self-indulgent. Freddie Lawrence's *The Easy Guide to*

Everyday Fitness and Successful Jogging cites the case of Ben, aged 41, and weighing in at 13 stone 4 lb, 'a good stone more than he should be according to his 5 foot 11 inch medium build. His job as a newspaper sub-editor means working under stress but involves little physical effort.' Ben, we are told, doesn't worry about his health. He gulps a casual breakfast, is driven to the station to catch a train, takes a bus to the office and the lift up.

At lunchtime he has three or four pints of beer, steak and kidney pie and chips. He smokes his way through the afternoon's work, takes two cakes off the refreshment trolley, and has two pints of beer before returning home on the train. On arrival he sinks into his armchair, has a whisky and a meal on a tray while watching television. The weekend is passed in a similar sedentary fashion with Ben unaware of the fact that he is probably asking for a heart attack. Ben is advised:

> To take stock of himself at this crucial point in his life and start making a few small but important changes in the way he lives; cutting down here, making an effort there. This will call for self-discipline, a battle with his prejudices and habits and a fresh look at his priorities. He needs to follow the basic rules of self servicing, remembering that regular exercise and a correct diet can add not only years to his life, but life to his years.

The slob is fat yet far from jolly. He belongs to

> a large group of people more prone to over-tiredness, shortness of breath, joint-swellings, arthritis, diabetes, gall-bladder disorders, hernias, high blood

pressure, varicose veins, kidney disease, backache —
and heart attacks.

Even worse:

Most of them look and feel their age, and if that
weren't enough, many of them suffer from mental
anguish, loss of mobility and a lack of self-
confidence. Being overweight is bad for the ego as
well as the heart.

'Are You', enquired Unity Hall in *The News of the
World*, 'Married to a Big Fat Slob?':

The worst slob I ever knew was a man who would
have a plate of hot sausages for his supper and
chomp through them while lying in bed reading a
racing paper in his vest. He couldn't believe it when
his wife left him.

Slobs, she went on to say, consider the use of deodor-
ants unmanly, 'moan about putting on fresh underwear or a clean shirt', and go to bed in their underwear.
A few weeks later she described the tremendous
response of women readers to her article: 'Most of
you are astonished that I described your husband so
accurately.' The campaign against the slob image was
joined by Marje Proops of *The Daily Mirror*: 'Until
now men have got away with it. "It" being their
bulging stomachs, flabby hips, spare tyre waists and
paunches.'
It was estimated that the average male is 10 lb
over-weight:

No wonder wives and girl friends look longingly at

lithe pop stars and trim muscular athletes and day-dream about lying beside them. Overweight men are almost always poor lovers and poor health risks.

Thirty-three years old, Brian Jacks, the judo Olympic medallist, joined in the chorus of reproach. Warning pot-bellies everywhere he had been described as the 'fittest man in Europe', he repeated the Health Education Council statement that Britain and America ranked low on the international fitness scale. Britain he said, is 'a land of pot-bellied men and wobbly-calved women', a situation he hopes to rectify through a company called Le Sport which has designed a new range of fitness equipment for a campaign described as 'Get Britain Fit'.

The purpose of fitness, we are now told, is to 'add more life to years, not just years to life'. Yet it is notoriously difficult to set minimum standards everyone can attain. Reduced to its basic advantages, regular exercise does lead to cardio-vascular improvement, enhanced physical work capacity and can reduce body fat, although there is no real substitute for dieting. And many experts have argued that the chief benefit of exercise is that you die fitter. Faced with the difficult problem of defining minimum standards of fitness applicable to people in all walks of life, propagandists fall back on the role appearance plays in our endless quest for social approval. 'Looking good' is professed to be the most tangible reward of physical effort. Not only will society benefit — we shall end up with a fitter nation — but more importantly the personal spin-offs include enhanced physical attractiveness and popularity. Those who do not make an effort are easily detectable — by their looks shall we know them. Those of us whose bodies exhibit the signs of middle-aged unfitness are clearly suffering from a self-inflicted wound. To look youthful is to be socially acceptable: and above all, to 'have fun'.

The importance of physical fitness in the middle years is nowhere more clearly exemplified than in the presidency of the United States. Publicists for the ex-filmstar, President Ronald Reagan, are at pains to disclaim the relevancy of his seventy years by drawing attention to the strength and colour of his hair and the vitality of his physical condition. Before his dramatic collapse on the jogging field in September 1979, Jimmy Carter's fitness for presidency was underwritten by his physician who claimed in *The New York Post* of 23 August 1979 he was as fit as a fiddle and 'can run faster now than he did in his college days'. Mr Carter himself said he had lost about 10 lb since he started his jogging regime about a year ago. His wife, too, joins him, and Rosalynn Carter at fifty-two has 'never looked better in her entire life. Unlike the consorts of others who have held high office, as "The First Lady" she showed none of the strains of being the President's wife.' Her relaxed and healthy appearance is the only fitting compliment to her sports enthusiast husband.

Jimmy Carter's physical collapse while jogging brought home the message that the benefits of exercise are not unmixed. In particular, the merits of jogging, one of the more recent popular mass pursuits, have been questioned on a number of grounds. Caution is advisable: you may, for instance, have a hidden health problem which sudden violent exercise could bring to crisis point. Of late, a number of jogging deaths have been reported in the press, one prominent victim being the England football team's doctor, 53-year-old Peter Burrows, a fitness fanatic. Medical experts have said that although Burrows appeared physically fit he was suffering from a serious build up of fatty deposits in the arteries. As a result of this and other tragedies it is recognized that strenuous exercise does not necessarily solve a serious health problem such as arteriosclerosis. If we look back on the life of the acrobatic film star Douglas Fairbanks we discern the same message.

Jogging is, of course, only the latest form of cheap mass exercise to have gripped the Western world. Originating in the States, where the best-seller lists are full of keep fit, jogging, and health maintenance manuals, its popularity has spread to Britain during the last five years. *The Sunday Times*, in a series of articles on 'Middle Age Fitness' in 1977 and 1978, encouraged readers to form jogging clubs, and *The Sun* and *The Daily Mirror* have both featured articles on 'jogging with the stars'. On 1 October 1978, *The Sunday Times* and British Heart Foundation-sponsored 'National Fun Run' took place, when nearly 12,000 joggers completed the three and a half mile course in Hyde Park. And there are numerous smaller versions of the National Fun Run. One of the pioneering authorities is the recreation department of Gateshead Council. The Olympic, European and Commonwealth medallist Brendan Foster, who runs the department, explained in his foreword to Cliff Temple's *Jogging for Fitness and Pleasure* how regular lunchtime jogging sessions were started at Gateshead in April 1975, when he was at first uncertain of the response. But:

Within a few weeks we were attracting as many as

150 people to each session, and the response emphasised what I have always maintained — that someone who has let himself get out of condition can find as much satisfaction in returning to a level of basic healthy fitness through a programme of jogging as an international athlete can get from winning a big race.

Also in 1978 the Sports Council backed the National Jogging Association's plans to promote jogging in Britain. The committee includes the managing editor of *Jogging Magazine* and its object is to encourage people to exercise responsibly to keep fit. On offer are information, promotion and mutual aids. Information is provided for the layman on jogging and other athletics and fitness schemes. There is an interest in encouraging the formation of jogging clubs and promoting the 'jogging message' to the whole population. The 'jogging message' is 'really the wider health and fitness message'. In the words of the secretary of the association:

One of the joys of jogging is that it's a personal, easy-to-do thing needing no rules or regulations. Another joy is that it's the ideal sociable activity. It's leading the trend in sport away from elite competition toward family-based fun. That's what it's all about nowadays.

Although many newspapers in Britain have given publicity to jogging and the general value of exercise for the middle aged there can be no doubt one of the most persistent campaigners under the banner of youth, fitness and beauty has been *The Sun* newspaper. In February 1979 it featured an adaptation of

Bruce Tulloh's book *The Complete Jogger*. Under the headline 'You Too Can Jog To Be 100', and alongside a photograph of two perky half-naked girls provocatively poised on a jogging machine, it announced: 'Everybody's at it! More than two million Britons are now staying fit and in shape by jogging. . . . And you don't have to feel left out because of advancing years.'

In January 1979, *The Sun* had attempted to whip up 'Keep Fit Fever'. It had also, the year before, run a 'Staying Alive Week', during which it asked 'superfit readers' to send in their bright ideas for fighting the flab. The top 100 entries received Health Education Council wall charts and teeshirts, and 400 runners-up received a wallchart. This national campaign sparked off a number of provincial imitations which similarly drew on the Health Education Council's definition of fitness, emphasizing that fitness can be fun. The fun concept is closely integrated with the youth, fitness and beauty message. Part of this links fitness with the ability to continue active life in some kind of sport, but above and beyond this practical message is the more elusive promise of sexual adventure or renewed vigour, and even undreamt of satisfactions. A central image, even when photographs of older men and women are included, is that of the firm, fresh, female body.

In August 1979, Bruce Tulloh was interviewed by Ian Wooldridge, sports writer for *The Daily Mail*. He said middle age was the time mortality began to make itself felt, 'the vulnerable age to potential joggers in that they are more aware of their lifespan'. Then, referring to Andrew Marvell's famous poem about 'Time's winged chariot hurrying near', he concluded on an interesting personal note: 'I can hear it rattling along behind me all the time. This is what keeps me going and I've certainly no intention of going before my time!' Some time previously Tulloh had written in *Jogging Magazine*:

> It is the person who allows the pressures to build up, and who never gets out of his grey tunnel into the real exciting world, who is being pushed to an early grave. The runner too, will have to go, sooner or later, more likely later, but until then he really can enjoy perpetual youth. This summer I went up a mountain with a man of 90 who was younger than many of my 35-year-old colleages.

Chronological age is not important, for exercise can make the middle-aged biologically younger. This doesn't make the body 'actually' become and look younger, but according to Tulloh 'The biggest bonus is the *feeling* of youthfulness that running gives us', and 'this feeling of youthfulness itself contributes to making us young.'

Certainly there is no absence of images of middle-aged people putting themselves, with various degrees of enthusiasm, under physical stress. The number of manuals dealing with jogging and other forms of exercise has grown apace. In America James F. Fix's *The Complete Book of Running* was on the best-seller list for over a year and other popular titles include J. Batten's *Complete Jogger* and J. Lillerfors' *Total Running*, and, explicitly for women, Kathryn Lance's *Running for Health and Beauty*. In Britain the US bestseller, Bob Glover and Jack Shepherd's *The Runner's Handbook*, was made available by Penguin. The authors claim:

> We are in the middle of a revolution. Suddenly,

in the mid-seventies, Americans by the tens of thousands are stripping off their clothes, pulling on shorts, lacing up shoes, and running. . . . They are running for their lives. They run because their friends are dropping dead from heart attacks. They run because they are fat, or scared or tense. They run because their lives are sedentary, made too easy by machines. As Dr Joseph Arends says, 'This is the Metallic Age. We have gold in our hearts, silver in our hair, and lead in our pants.'

Popular titles by British authors include Freddie Lawrence's *The Easy Guide to Everyday Fitness and Successful Jogging*. Freddie Lawrence is chief information officer of the Health Education Council and was manager of the national 'Look After Yourself Campaign'. He is thirty-eight and describes his own pursuit of fitness 'as a never ending battle between good and evil'.

Health educationalists, physical fitness experts, and allied enthusiasts do not disguise the fact that routine exercise demands discipline and hard work. To sugar the pill they normally advise the middle aged to awaken their sluggish bodies cautiously and usually not before they have had a medical check-up. Notwithstanding the occasional cautionary tale the benefits are allegedly prodigious. *The Easy Guide to Everyday Fitness and Successful Jogging* typically addresses itself to the reader who 'almost certainly' already knows he is not as fit as he could be. Typically he will be middle aged, the kind of person who can easily call to mind:

The old days when you were younger, felt more agile and looked quite something in those slim-fit clothes you can't wear now. When there were less of those vague but irritating aches and pains and you could dance all night.

The cover shows a slim, blond girl in a trim jogging outfit of scarlet shorts and neat teeshirt with the 'Look After Yourself' emblem across it — a round, bald, skipping cartoon figure. In vain pursuit is a chubby suited man in his late twenties or early thirties: 'Improve your sex life.' 'Regain your health and vitality.' 'How to slow the ageing process and live longer.' 'Look and feel younger.' 'Improve your figure.' 'Stop the sagging stomach.' 'Prevent creeping obesity.' 'Eat better, sleep better, feel better, look better.' 'Add years to your life and life to your years.' On the back cover our man has caught up with the girl and is leading her with a backward triumphant smile into the night.

The youth and beauty connection seems inescapable. Exercise is urged on the middle aged precisely because it can bring about alterations to appearance. Indeed, as we have noted, these external changes are a more certain outcome than longevity. Improved health, as the history of many a recidivist 'fatty' shows, is often an inadequate motive to persist. Social approval, exhortation, and support is indispensable and an enhanced physical appearance is the surest way to recognition of effort. So, in *Jogging Magazine* for March 1980, a young healthy bright-eyed girl with long shining hair, and dressed in a jogging outfit, smiles invitingly out. Under a caption 'What Jogging Does for Your Body', we are told it 'Puts you in control of your body, improves confidence, increases psychological well-being'; 'Improves circulation, essential for clear complexion'; 'Improves quality of

107

sleep, gives eyes that "sparkle" '; 'Improves posture:
no more drooping and sagging'; 'Strengthens the
pectoral muscles, firms up the bust'; 'Promotes good
breathing practices, reduces stomach movement and
sag'; 'Helps burn off excess fat and cellulite, firms up
thighs'. In an accompanying article entitled 'Jogging
Sounds Fine, But Won't It Make Me Muscley?',
Margaret McLoughlin contests the view that women
could end up with unsightly muscles: 'Listen: jogging,
cycling, keep-fit — they're all accepted parts of every
beauty regime.' Referring to the fact that many of
the Miss World competition contestants were keen
joggers, she adds: 'These girls have got to have beautiful figures. And if exercise were bad for the shape,
they wouldn't be doing it, would they?'

Dr Frank Newton, a prominent member of the
British Association of Sport and Medicine, agrees that
jogging makes women look good and feel good:

> I'm not going to say that jogging will instantly
> transform a woman into Brigitte Bardot. But I will
> say that I've noticed over the years that the women
> who start to jog with our club do experience a
> definite improvement in their looks. . . . After a
> few weeks you can definitely see an improvement.
> There's a smile on the face, the eyes are shining,
> the expression is cheerful. The women look 100 per
> cent better. Even in such a short space of time her
> figure seems to have improved.

Another article in the March 1979 issue of *Jogging
Magazine* features Lesley Watson, one of Britain's
leading marathon runners. 'When you jog it's
important not only to feel good but to look good.'
When she prepares to go training for a race she puts

on mascara and a splash of Rive Gauche perfume. Thirty-year-old Lesley, described in *The Sun* as 'Britain's Wonder Woman', says she always wears track-suit leggings even in the summer on training runs:

Officially it's to keep my muscles warm and prevent pulls but really I don't like people to see my lily-white legs. I'm afraid I'm so vain that I even put tan make-up on them when I compete.

In the July edition of *Jogging Magazine*, 51-year-old ex-model Shirley Kennedy describes how she gave up athletics after school because her father thought women athletes were too muscley. This she now feels was foolish for: 'In fact, running keeps you slim. It definitely dulls the appetite and it also firms up my thighs. I think its a great beauty aid.'

8

Looking Good and Feeling Great II:

SLIMMING AND COSMETIC SURGERY

Women, especially younger women, have always
been expected to take care of their looks. But in the
past men were conditioned not to scrutinize themselves too closely, especially as they grew older. The
masculine virtues did not include vanity or narcissism.
Since the last war, however, men have come under
greater pressure to take care of the face and body.
Even in the Victorian period, which saw the first
uneasy stirrings of body-consciousness in the middle-
aged male, self-monitoring was recommended largely
in the larger interests of society and the pursuit of
spiritual perfection. It was important to keep fit to
perform the conventional duties of the solid, respectably 'mature', citizen. Women too, as we have seen,
were not expected to disguise the physical effects of
ageing entirely but to transform them gracefully into
the proud symbols of post-menopausal dignity. The
growth of consumer culture has tended to erode these
conventions and replace them with the concept of the
body 'natural', contained in the modern theory of the
social value of appearances. Charles Hix writes in his
recent male guide *Looking Good*, that we usually:

Think of physical fitness in terms of health. Certainly a fit body looks good, and looking good is almost always associated with good health. Men whose bodies are physically fit will probably perform better even when weakened by physical illness, than so-called healthy men who have allowed their bodies to go to pot. A sedentary person can be healthy, meaning not ill, but is his body fit? Diagnostically, he's not perhaps wracked with disease, practically, his physical fitness is a mirage.

Clothes, he warns, do not make the man: the clothes you wear cannot change your visible physique.

For those who don't want to don a jogging suit there are pleasanter ways of keeping fit. Under the headline 'Slimline Tonic: Jog and Snog', *The Daily Mirror* noted:

Jogging is becoming a cult activity. But there's an even more popular way to keep fit — making love. The sex act uses up about 200 calories. You'd have to jog for half an hour to work that off. Doctor Barnard says making love regularly three times a week can trim off about four pounds. Sex, he says, equals twenty press-ups, and he recommends it for those who can get no other form of exercise.

Almost three months later in 'What a Lovely Way to Slim' the prominent *Sun* columnist on health and beauty, Sally Anne Voak, publicized Richard Smith's book, *The Dieter's Guide to Weight Loss during Sex*. Smith is an American writer 'who has spent two years producing a comprehensive calorie-guide to sex and

111

sexy activities like kissing, caressing and tickling your partner'. His book of 'fun-advice' has sold thousands of copies in America, where it was at the top of the best-sellers' list. Smith, thirty-seven and single, rates food, diet, sex and human behaviour as his favourite subjects. He claims to have discovered that sex is a more efficient way of burning up calories than jogging, or playing tennis, or swimming, etc. He says slimming experts believe a regular and active sex life can tone up thigh and tummy muscles and cut down cravings for 'comfort' foods like sweets, booze and puddings, which are all very fattening. He provides a humorous breakdown of the number of calories burned in almost every activity it is possible to associate with the erotic, including preparation for the bedroom, showering, brushing teeth, telling dirty jokes, fumbling (94 calories), French and Dutch kissing, and unhooking bras (with hands steady or trembling).

Unlike the Victorians, who believed that bodily desires were important only in as far as they served a higher spiritual purpose, we find it difficult to imagine an existence in which the body plays less than a central role. At the heart of the modern theory of the body 'natural' are prescriptions for combating the visible signs of ageing in the cosmetic interests of youth, fitness and beauty. The dominant Western concept is now of the body, not as a vehicle for the soul, but as a piece of machinery without which 'life', as we understand it, is meaningless. The consequence is that ageing is more than ever seen to be symptomatic of breakdown and disease, and a sign of negligence, indiscipline, and disuse which can only lead to exclusion from the finer things of life. The more emphasis we place on the virtues of holding the

112

physical signs of ageing at bay, the greater will be the tensions we experience in middle age.

In *The Daily Mirror* of 20 April 1977, Chris Hutchings told the inside story of how sweat and surgery made Tom Jones a living legend. It cost he said, £6,000 for every pound in weight Jones lost. In 1966 he weighed 15 stone, had a double chin, a broken nose resulting from a fight, ate large quantities of stodgy food, drank large quantities of beer, and his son's sixteenth birthday brought home to him the possibility he could be a grandfather at the age of thirty-three. A combined operation was launched to reduce his body and to transform his face. His diet changed to champagne and steaks. A leisure complex was built in the garden of his home, where he trained assiduously and reduced his weight to 11 stone 5 lb, the lightest he had been since he was twelve years old. The health coach at Caesar's Palace at Las Vegas now says Tom is fitter than any man he knows. He had a nose job in 1967 and an operation to tighten the skin under his jaw in 1972. Because this operation is not permanent he had to have another one two years later.

Weight reduction has a central part to play in any fitness campaign. One thing the fit person is not is a fat slob. The Health Education Council asserts we should not, generally speaking, weigh more at any age than we did in our twenties. In our twenties our bodies are on average firmer and slimmer. It was not then surprising that the HEC should choose the traditional image of the middle-aged man, so rounded and balding he can easily be caricatured as a ball of fat which must needs be skipped, jogged and otherwise exercised away, as the emblem for the English 'Look After Yourself' campaign of 1978.

Men, it is widely believed, are relatively unaffected by the modern obsession with slimming. Whilst it is certainly true that the membership of slimming clubs is largely made up of women, there is no evidence that overweight men are immune to the general stigma attached to obesity and sometimes the result is tragic. One man who had his teeth wired together in a desperate attempt to lose weight managed to reduce from 20 to 11½ stones. From being a fat, happy man, his wife recalled, he became thin and miserable. He now had a new image to live up to and temporarily left home with a 16-year-old girl, who told him 'what a marvellous new person he was'. After returning he found it increasingly difficult to keep his weight down and finally died when he insisted surgeons should reverse the operation he had undergone to reduce the size of his stomach.

Fat men, of course, have always had tragi-comic appeal. Roscoe 'Fatty' Arbuckle created one of the enduring images of the fat man isolated from the world of his slimmer fellows. Oliver 'Babe' Hardy, whose size helped create the enduring partnership of Laurel and Hardy, worried all his life about his weight. He was a big man, over 6 ft tall, weighing at his heaviest 350 lb, and extremely self-conscious about his appearance. His clothes, always made to measure, were meticulously tailored: there was nothing, he felt, worse than seeing a fat man carelessly dressed.

One of the ways we become aware of our bodies is when we discover they are perceived by others to be abnormal. In these poignant moments we see ourselves as others see us and in the columns of slimming magazines women testify incessantly to the tragicomedy of obesity. One woman reported that although married to an uncritical husband, and certainly not obese, she became very self-conscious and never went out. One day she forced herself to go to her brother's wedding and the ensuing photograph gave her the biggest shock of her life. It confirmed her worst fears and speeded her into a slimming club. She never dared admit to herself she was overweight until she drew attention to an enormously fat woman and her husband replied she was twice her size. Looking back from the vantage point of a fuller social life she recalled her husband had never mentioned her increasing size yet they no longer went out anywhere together. Others who have been fat from childhood remember how much they were hurt by jeering schoolmates and the social isolation they endured. Outsize clothing did not disguise their fat; it merely covered up the offending flesh. Others remember that their size was a disappointment to their parents, and even brothers and sisters would sometimes refuse to speak to them.

Ostensibly, of course, we stigmatize obesity because it it dangerous to health, an unmistakable indication of over-indulgence. Regular consumption of large numbers of calories, especially from middle age onwards, when the body requires less and will only store them as fat, is associated with a number of specific diseases. Yet, as is the case of physical fitness, the health motive is ultimately less significant socially than the cosmetic one. Obesity experts frequently stress that apart from an unfortunate minority of cases, obesity is often a social rather than a purely medical issue. In the public image, fatness is linked with failure and low social status. Top people are slim and lovely, handsome and fit, and when they fail to live up to this image are not infrequently reminded of their shortcomings. Recently, Princess Margaret was congratulated for losing weight. In her article 'Margaret's Slimline Tonic', Audrey Whiting wrote:

> After bleak months of illness and emotional up-heaval she has slimmed down, toned up and got herself fighting fit and raring to go. Not so long ago she was overweight, unwell and unhappy. Now she is a new woman.

A photograph shows Princess Margaret returning from holiday in August 1976 after her marriage break up. She looks overweight and unhappy. Subsequently she subjected herself to a strict food and health regime:

> As she improved physically, companions noticed a change in her mental approach. She was no longer constantly tense and uptight. Friends began to enjoy her company again.

Even more heroic was the account of Elizabeth Taylor's fight to lose weight presented in the popular media. In May 1979, *The Daily Mirror* drew the attention of its readers to her matronly appearance. At forty-seven the famous film star had 'lost the bloom of youth'. Not to be outdone *The Sun* exclaimed 'OH LIZ! She is losing the Battle of the Bulge in a big way.' The camera, we were reliably informed, did not lie: 'This bloated, triple-chinned matron IS Liz Taylor.' The usually flattering 'before and after' treatment was reversed in an enlarged photograph of Liz 'rapidly losing her battle to shed gross layers of fat'. A small snapshot of her 1976 face showed her 'Slim and full of vitality'. In the past, it said, 'She has always managed to slim down whenever her weight soared from stuffing herself with good food. But her latest battle against the bulge has not worked.' Friends feared she had an illness, but a front-page report in *The Daily Mirror* of 16 July 1979 brought the good news: 'THIN LIZZY — She's Taylor made again.' She was now slimmer and fitter than she'd been for months. A close friend said she'd had a miserable time for years trying to keep her weight down 'But she's eating a lot less now'. The political fund-raising dinners she had attended in support of her husband had played havoc with her figure though her sacrifice of film star curves helped him to win a seat in the US Senate.

To *Sun* readers on Wednesday, 18 July 1979, she spoke 'exclusively'. Alongside a 'before and after' photograph of 'Tubby Taylor and Slimline Liz', she renounced the world of glamour and Hollywood: 'I don't think about the way I look now.' Her transformation was, she revealed, accomplished at the £80 a day Pompano Beach health spa near Miami Beach where she eliminated fat on a 600 calorie daily diet, jogging, swimming, ballet and herbal baths. She had been urged by friends to trim and had received a large number of letters from fans urging her not to let herself go. 'The last straw came in February, when Liz was guest of honour at a posh charity dinner in New York's Waldorf Astoria hotel. She stormed out when a comedian joked about her weight and booked into the exclusive health farm.'

On Friday, 20 July *The Daily Mirror* announced that she had been awarded the title 'special slimmer of the month'. The article stressed that few of us can afford to go to the kind of health farm she used, but 'it is possible to have a health-farm-type weekend in your own home for next to nothing'. Here the importance of strengthening the slimmer's resolve through the participation of a relative, loved one, or neighbour, was emphasized, 'The feeling of all being in the same boat is what keeps people on the straight and narrow at expensive health farms'. The rest of the article went on to detail the approved regime. Not to be outdone *The Sun* of 7 August exclusively proclaimed 'THE DIET THAT IS TAYLOR MADE FOR SUN READERS'. Again the article described Liz's diet and promised that readers could follow 'the same magic diet'. Unlike the *Mirror*, *The Sun* detailed her diet of high protein, costing around £1,700 for 21 days. But the additional attraction was that two readers were offered the chance to try Liz's cure at Palm Aire if they could tell the editor which tempting foods stopped them from successful slimming and which foods they enjoyed the most.

All slimming and exercise regimes are recommended on the grounds that followers will experience a change in appearance and such a change is always for the better. Thus the miner who lost several stones because his daughter was upset when her schoolmates laughed at his appearance is photographed comically engulfed by his old trousers. Those who wish to publicize the benefits must not only describe them in print but publish photographs to demonstrate they are real. In *The Daily Mirror* for 31 August 1978, for example, the story of the struggles of John and Linda Jenkins, who spent six months fighting the flab 'that made romance very heavy going', is dominated by a 'before and after' photograph under the headline 'Losing Oodles Means Canoodles'. After transforming themselves from two paunchy, homely figures to a slim, fashionably dressed couple they were voted 'Slimmers of 1978' by *Slimming Magazine*. Shortly afterwards they appeared in a two-page colour advertisement for Slimcea calorie-reduced bread. A poster on display in bread shops showed them stretched out on a sunny beach: The girl who said she could never dare wear a bikini 'will tell you, less calories can lead to a lot more fun!'

The 1979 *Slimming Magazine* slimmer of the year was even more sensational: a 35-year-old woman who had weighed 28 stone 12 lb and lost 'an astonishing 18 stone'. 'Never before in the history of this premiere titled contest have we been able to bring you such an amazing, inspiring story.' Describing her struggle and eventual triumph over flab she said she had now freed both her husband and herself from a dragging misery, 'Before I lost 18 stone, I never dreamed I could look normal let alone pretty'. Valerie, slimmer of the year, was also glamorously posed in a double-page advert for Slimcea bread.

The cosmetic significance of slimming is most completely realized in the 'before and after' comparisons made in slimming magazines and by slimming clubs. It is not simply that obesity and overweight are stigmatized but that a slim appearance is extolled as the acme of perfection, efficiency, and all-purpose 'fun'. A *News of the World* article about an ordinary middle-aged couple confirmed this view. Under the headline 'Sheila's Flabby Love Life Gets a Slimline Tonic', it told how 40-year-old mother of three Sheila went down from 13 to 9 stone after joining a weight watchers club and her 41-year-old husband demonstrated renewed ardour:

He brings me surprise parcels of sexy underwear now. And he's coming home in his lunch hour . . . and not because of the quality of the food. Sometimes we'll be watching television and I can feel him looking at me. I know what he's thinking and it makes me feel like a 16-year-old again.

The husband added, however, that she was so full of energy he was worried she would wear him out and had to take vitamin pills and do exercises to keep fit. Summing up the advantages of her changed lifestyle Sheila observed:

When you feel more attractive, you naturally become more enthusiastic. So Allen and I now go dancing and swimming, and are even thinking of taking up golf. It's like starting a new life.

An inner state of health is ideally mirrored in shining hair, sparkling eyes, dazzling teeth, and athletically extended limbs and torso, photographically frozen in positions the unfit are probably unable to hold. Thus the photographic model, obviously basking in approval and having fun, is 'living proof' it pays to be slim. Recently area organizers of Weight Watchers have reported strong request from members over twenty who 'would like some fashion and beauty hints just for them', who have therefore been included in 'befores and afters'. Although they have used young models they have tried to show clothes that 'can be worn by any age group'. Although directed at women of all ages, the ideal type of female beauty is portrayed as soft, feminine, and romantic. Thus Joanna helps Madeline 'choose clothes suitable for her life' and Madeline is a 'delectably pretty girl with long legs, slim body and a most desirably curving bosom'. Attractive Catherine enjoys borrowing her 15-year-old daughter's trendy fashions; and vice versa because 'When Cathy goes fashion shopping it's for T-shirts to tuck into jeans, high-style cords and boots — and the wolf whistles she gets confirm her confidence in her new found good looks.' There are countless other examples; the point is that mother and daughter attempt to merge youthful identities by wearing similar or shared clothing, and both are equally keen to attract the admiring attention of strange men.

In all the major slimming magazines the pleasures and rewards of slender femininity are expanded into a complete lifestyle. One does not slim for health's sake alone. Continuity between beautiful personal appearance and enjoyment of a total way of life is perpetually reaffirmed. In the homelier slimming magazines the techniques are simple and straightforward: new calorie-free recipes, picnics, play snacks, DIY, energetic gardening, housework and happy family pursuits. The overall image here is of happy families united in an active home life. By contrast, the avowed aim of the glossy, sophisticated *Playgirl* kind of approach is complete freedom of self-expression and zestful hedonism. Beautiful women are often portrayed lost in solitary self-admiration, caressing and enjoying the feel of their own bodies. This narcissistic approach contrasts sharply with the traditional housewifely role. In the words of the publishers:

We have tried to give you, our reader, what *you* want, both photographically and editorially. . . . Above all we try to reinforce the fact that you are vibrant and beautiful beings deserving of whatever entertainment pleases you.

121

The homelier magazines gear their recruitment programmes to the domestic role and carefully spell out ways in which it can be enhanced. On the front cover of *Slimmer Silhouette* is the image of a young attractive woman in workmanlike kitchen apron serving up meat and two veg — a slimming meal of chicken, mushrooms and peas. Dawne's husband was thrilled when he came home from sea to find she had lost nearly 4 stones and 'become a willowly glamour girl'. When he sailed away Dawne weighed 12 stones and felt embarrassed by her body. At first he didn't recognize her but is now delighted to have a slim wife. 'It's true', Greg confirmed, 'I want to show her off all the time. I'm so proud I'm always trying to persuade her to wear her tightest trousers! Looking so good, she has become far more confident, more outgoing.' Dawne also went jogging, did exercises and joined a health club. She and Greg have bought racing bikes and spend every spare moment cycling through the lanes near their home town. They are also buying a home on a brand-new estate.

Slimming allegedly accelerates the pace of life in whatever social group we belong to. As Ruth Rose, twenty-eight, of Sale put it 'Being overweight was, for me, like living with the brakes on. And I *hated* being held back.' Ruth can now wear her swimsuit with confidence. The pace is fastest, of course, for Playgirls and Playboys. According to a youthful-looking Ira E. Ritter, publisher and chairman of the *Playgirl* board, 'Every woman wants a better body; your present active life requires it.' Although 'we are not here to tell you to look, dress and act like anyone else or model your figure after skinny cover girls' and 'life can't be lived between the pages of a glamour magazine', their glossy 'Diet and Exercise' booklet, does claim to share the lifestyle of the beautiful people with its readers. On page 13, Franchesco Scavulo, one of the world's top fashion photographers, explains 'how beautiful people stay lean'. Born in 1929, the busy photographer has more energy than most people half his age. 'People tell me how healthy and vital I look. When we talk about my diet they become interested.' Scavulo, an avowed enemy of fat, which he belives is completely unnatural and out of place in the world of fashion — 'We are not supposed to be fat' — offers a number of tips for 'slender eating' and is not the only man to be found in these pages.

Outstanding slimmer is Dr Larry Reich, who was a fat kid and grew fatter. His overeating came to an end in 1972 when he was a prisoner in Uganda and he now weighs 162 lb and models clothes for a chic gentleman's quarterly. Dr Reich's approach is psychological rather than dietary and includes the following recommendations: 'Cut out a picture of the body you would like to have and put a photo of your head on it. Attach it to the inside of the refrigerator door'; 'As your weight goes down, get rid of your "fat" clothes. You don't want to invest a lot of money, but you can either have your old clothes altered or buy some new old clothes that are fun to wear, or buy some jeans'; 'Put a mirror on the outside of the refrigerator door'; 'Find a "trusted other". Someone you admire and respect, with whom you can share your goals, who will be supportive and can enjoy your success with you.' And *Playgirl* adds this advice: 'Have a photo taken of your naked posterior — keep it on your desk or secrete it away in your wallet to be viewed just before you're about to buy a piece of mousse.'

Perhaps the last word on slimming for the masses

should come from Jean Nidetch, founder of the staggeringly successful Weight Watchers empire. Describing herself as a 'formerly fat housewife' weighing over 200 lb and a failed dieter once married to a 'formerly fat bus driver', her main advice is always that there is no more compelling reason to lose weight than vanity:

> Vanity is the major reason people want to lose weight. I, for one, could never get all choked up about the health benefits of proper eating habits. I never cared about nutrition. But I did care about how I looked.

Is it all worth it, we ask?

> Well, I go to the beach and I'm not embarrassed in a bathing suit. I always was before. I go shopping and I buy whatsoever clothes I like. I never could before. I enjoy tennis and I'm learning to play golf. Would I have been seen on a tennis court or a golf course before?

Rightly cautious, she offers no cast-iron guarantee that losing weight automatically produces a 'beautiful' life or immediate success:

> But *surely* it's going to make you confident that you are capable of controlling your own body, that you are not a helpless victim.

The reason, of course, the slimming industry is so successful is that the world is full of failed dieters and the many people for whom the ascetic daily disciplines of perennially youthful stars have no attraction. One way of having our cake and eating it is to give our bodies a regular service at one of the many health farms which have sprung up over the last few years. As *Mirror* readers were told, the expensive health farm Elizabeth Taylor visited was well beyond the reach of most of us and the cheap homely version readers were encouraged to try with the help of a friend, neighbour or spouse is really nothing like an expensive health farm which has a lifestyle all of its own. It's a world of luxuriously appointed fittings, ever-present attendants, and costly advice which includes guidance on psychological and other life matters. A far cry from the humble version recommended by this popular daily newspaper is the elaborate regime at the famous Golden Door in Escondido, California, where, in the words of novelist Kathrin Perutz, 'Women tired of the world, their bodies, or husbands could make a retreat and return refreshed.' In addition to a wide range of rejuvenating treatments the Golden Door offers a philosophy one is unlikely to find in a small private 'health club' in a provincial town, say in the north of England. Even so, one of these can typically claim:

> You don't have to go to an exclusive health farm to use Salon 20. Salon 20, a new machine . . . complete with 20 pads covers the entire body comfortably tones up flabby muscles and used in conjunction with a controlled diet, helps you lose weight from different places, thighs, buttocks and hips, etc.

A shorter cut to youthful appearance is cosmetic surgery. Despite a 1930s prediction by Helena Rubinstein, who expected her combined treatment of exercise and cosmetics would short circuit the need for cosmetic surgery, it has proved increasingly attractive to women and men and is now an accepted feature of the complete health, fitness and beauty regime. 'Cosmetic' differs from 'plastic surgery' in so far as the latter attempts to reconstruct parts of the face or conspicuous parts of the body so obviously disfigured by accident or disease they interfere with normal social life. Cosmetic surgery is more than an attempt to help a person look 'normal'. In the words of the great pioneering surgeon Sir Harold Gillies, it 'is an attempt to surpass the normal'.

Sometimes called 'beauty' or 'aesthetic surgery', it first found popularity with society women during the years immediately following World War I. Thanks to technical advances in reconstructing the faces of men disfigured in the trenches, 'face-lifting' — a luxurious operation for women who could afford to have their wrinkles stretched away — became safer and more effective. Surgical techniques, developed to bring comfort to the sick and injured, could now profitably be used to remove (at least temporarily) some of the more obvious natural signs of ageing. Then, as now, it was necessary to seek out a reputable surgeon if one wished to avoid the horrors of a botched face lift. The famous *New Faces — New Futures*, published in the US in 1936 by Dr Maxwell Maltz, established the tradition of warning prospective clients against the increasing number of charlatans. Face lifting could only 'change the whole course of life' for the better if carried out by accredited surgeons. First check, therefore, with a doctor or the American Medical Association before submitting to the knife. The trouble was that, because cosmetic surgery was in its infancy, competent practitioners were not too easy

126

to find. Maltz estimated there were 12 to 14 in Britain, in France a like number, 10 to 12 in Germany, in Italy 4, and in the United States, 40 or 50. At least for the fortunate few, beauty in middle age really could be 'skin deep'.

Improvements in technique do not fully account for the present-day popularity of cosmetic surgery. Increasing demand is a response to the value placed on grooming and appearance in our materialistic society. Before the last war, cosmetic surgery was a novel procedure which, despite its acceptance in fashionable circles, was not generally regarded as respectable and indeed was often discussed only in a whisper by women who approached the consulting rooms of even reputable surgeons by the back door. Whilst the moderate use of cosmetics to improve on nature was increasingly acceptable, attempts to interfere directly with normal (and inevitable) physical changes were regarded with considerable suspicion. It is still the case today that some celebrities who publicly parade their cosmetic, diet and exercise regimes fight shy of admitting they have had cosmetic surgery. Yet all this is changing. 'You can', said the *TV Times* in November 1979, 'read about the fast developing and increasingly accepted work of the cosmetic surgeons and how they are helping more and more men and women.' Three prizes of £1,000 worth of cosmetic surgery could be won which 'could take years off you' – an optimistic note now also found in many other popular papers which, even though they usually echo the cautionary tones of Maxwell Maltz years before, project a breezy image of cosmetic surgery. Thus *The Sun* speaks of 'the cosmetic surgery boom that is giving thousands of people an exciting new outlook on life'. The next paragraph of ballyhoo reads, 'Stars galore have turned to surgeons in their search for better looks and more beautiful bodies. Most have succeeded.' Professor Ivo Pitanguy, beauty surgeon to the stars, in keeping with his professional standards, is duly cautious in making extravagant claims for cosmetic surgery yet has to acknowledge:

> Society today gives much importance to youth and good looks. Appearances play a large part in social competition. You can be in possession of bodily health, but not have a sense of well-being about your looks. If I can make you a happier man by giving you this sense of satisfaction — why not.

Long before the British 'boom' of the late 1970s, cosmetic surgery was big business in the States where an aggressive entrepreneurial spirit created the cosmetic surgery success story. Journalists and surgeons joined forces to combine sober descriptions of surgical procedures with exuberant celebrations of the American dream. Typical of the genre is Smith and Sinclair Baker's *Doctor Make Me Beautiful*. The aim of this book, addressed both to women and men, is 'Not to discuss the subject of facial and body correction and improvement abstractly, *but to help you to a better future*'. An emphasis is on happy and successful living, now made more possible than ever thanks to technical advances. There is, we are told, no need to apologize for being concerned about our appearance.

The good news, say the authors, is that the cultivation of appearance has been given the seal of approval by the American Medical Association's committee on cosmetics:

Good personal appearance is important to self-confidence and to the esteem needed by young and old alike. Cosmetics excel in helping women to make the most of their appearance. Skilfully used, cosmetics can modify the external appearance to overcome minor blemishes, and add colour.

And second, they say, that cosmetic plastic surgery is the most effective method of eliminating the undesirably facial characteristics of ageing in both sexes:

The face lift can correct wrinkles of the cheek; the sagging of the skin into jowls which can cause loss of the firm youthful outline of the lower jaw or mandible; the deepening of the groove of the outer nostril of the nose to the angle of the mouth; the groove from the angle of the mouth to the border of the lower jaw which creates a doughnut-circumoral pattern; the wrinkled skin that sags under the chin and forms cords from the skin down to the chest; and the folds of the 'turkey gobbler' falling from the chin to mid-neck.

The bad news is that it's a disgrace to show, in middle age, one is growing old. Ageing is unattractive and therefore undesirable. No attempt is made to question the view that men and women who look their age are less satisfactory employees, marriage partners, lovers, celebrities, or national leaders. To allow marks of the passage of time to remain, once one has been alerted to their presence, is to fail to harness the considerable energies remaining in middle age to the necessary competitive struggle to look young both at home and at work.

'Where America leads,' it is often said, 'the rest of

the world will follow.' And there is no doubt this particular manifestation of the American pioneering spirit has successfully crossed the Atlantic. Cautionary tales and words of warning have had little effect on the 'British boom' in cosmetic surgery. Indeed, one of the greatest problems plastic surgeons have to contend with is the patient who expects post-operative life to improve dramatically. Myra, 46, had faith in the miracle of cosmetic surgery. Newly divorced and totally lacking in confidence in herself, she spent nearly £3,000 on facial and body surgery:

I really believed that operation was my lifeline. I started dreaming about it when my husband was having an affair with the girl he has now married. She was a lot younger than me, and I really thought I could buy back my youth. I had my eyes done, which was a success and a face lift which no-one but me ever noticed. I also had the tummy tuck to get rid of my stretch marks. But when it was over I went into a really bad depression, partly because of having three general anaesthetics, and obviously because my general situation hadn't changed. I don't think it was a waste of money. But I do think the doctor I went to in Manchester should have talked to me much more seriously about my motives for what I was doing.

The glossy women's magazine *Company* recently reported that medical columnists receive more letters about nose-jobs and boobs than anything else. One important reason for the British boom in cosmetic surgery, said *The Daily Express*, is the belief that it can arrest the natural ageing process. *The Daily Mirror* tells us the cosmetic surgery business is also booming in America as millions line up to the 'kindest cut of all'. More and more ordinary citizens are undergoing cosmetic surgery and the United States government allows the cost of cosmetic surgery to be tax deductible because after it people tend to remain at work longer. In Britain, hundreds of ordinary people are spending their savings in private plastic surgery clinics where prices range from £350 to £1,500 (the cheaper mini-lift, popular with those in their thirties, currently costs around £350). Many men and women are having these operations to cope with the ravages of time.

Thus the cost of surgery has not acted as a deterrent. Hair transplants, brow lifts, eyelid jobs, ear flap work, nose, chin lifts, full-face lifts, breast reduction or enlargement, tummy tucks, bottom lifts, and even subtler variations are not usually provided 'free' by the National Health Service for purely cosmetic purposes. The cause of any defect must be accident, injury, or illness before it will be surgically corrected at the State's expense − or there must at least be evidence of serious psychological disturbance. 'All the operations to make you look younger', warned *The News of the World*, 'are only available in private clinics.' Because the results vary from person to person, clients are often advised to combine surgical treatment with a changed hairstyle, new clothes and new cosmetic techniques. The 'before and after' photographs of successful facial plastic surgery usually show changes in hairstyle, make-up and clothing, some of which would probably have had a rejuvenating effect anyway. In September 1979, columnist Katharine Whitehorn reflected on the fact that enormous numbers of women now wanted to have something done about their appearance. After

131

an article on face lifts appeared in *Woman's Own* there were 7,000 letters asking for addresses of clinics. She added that *The Sun* regularly received 5 per cent of its advice letters on this subject. Agony columnist Claire Rayner, an ex-nurse, had informed her she is now convinced after several thousand letters that the nose or bosom job really does do what the sufferer hopes it will do.

In an article entitled: 'You and the Cult of Youth: Now It's Men Who Are Having Their Faces Lifted', Vicki MacKenzie examined the case of Mike Miller, aged 37, the catering manager of a London car firm, who explained why he saved £700 for his 'face job':

> I was anxious of what I *might* look like when I'm middle aged. I didn't think I could afford to wait, financially or psychologically for another ten years. The more I considered it the more urgent a face lift became. I did it for my own satisfaction. To keep me looking at my best for as long as I can. Well, if you look good, you feel good.

The article pointed out Mike Miller was by no means unique: a growing number of middle-class men (salesmen, advertising men, dentists, accountants, etc.) are going in for cosmetic surgery offered by the new cut-price cosmetic surgery clinics which operate a quick turnover business and keep their prices down to about £400. This upsurge of male cosmetic surgery has taken place within the last five years and is almost catching up with the numbers of women. Most of the men who have surgery are aged forty to fifty.

The month after Katharine Whitehorn had written that *The Sun* seldom published articles on cosmetic surgery, a series 'The Beauty Makers', describing an increase in the numbers of people seeking cosmetic surgery, appeared. Harris Austin, co-owner of the Park Clinic in London, said the demand for plastic surgery had grown over the last twelve years and although they didn't do National Health Service work most of their consultants worked for the NHS. '99 per cent of our customers are ordinary people, rather than the rich and famous, and they all come privately.' One of their most popular operations, breast augmentation, is popularly known as 'the Spring Special because women rush for them so that they can fill out their bikinis on the summer beaches'. 'Today', commented *The Sun*, 'when youth means sexuality and success, more and more ordinary women are having operations.' But it has also been estimated that one client in four in Britain is a man. Grahame Storer, director of the Grahame Allan centre in Manchester, reported that men get worried over hair loss or wrinkles and some want the operation done because they are working with younger men. One reason why private clinics are becoming more popular is the increasing waiting list for NHS clinics. In 1977, the latest year for which the Department of Health and Social Security has figures, there were 46,000 plastic and cosmetic surgery operations performed, taking up 1,725 of the Health Service 80,000 beds. There was a waiting list of 35,000, more than half of whom had been waiting for more than a year, and the list is lengthening daily. For those who can't raise the money for private cosmetic surgery, the Cosmetic Surgery Finance Scheme was started in 1979 to provide loans of up to £1,500 payable at 14 per cent over 2 years. What emerges from this assorted information is that it is now acceptable to talk openly about plastic surgery and raise money to have it.

More and more people who don't have serious psychological problems or physical stigmata are demanding cosmetic surgery. It seems also clear that cosmetic surgery is increasingly respectable because the stereotype of youth and vitality is alive and well.

Nevertheless, in comparison with the States, the publicity in Britain still remains relatively muted. An enterprising publisher has yet to seize the opportunity to commission a British equivalent to *Doctor Make Me Beautiful*, or Simona Morini's *Body Sculpture: Plastic Surgery from Head to Toe*. Throughout the country, private cosmetic surgery clinics advertise their services in brochures usually giving only sketchy descriptions of their most popular procedures. The Sister Rose organization, for example, has a network of health care clinics and consulting facilities from Glasgow to London. Attention is drawn to the careful medical supervision of all procedures and the clinics are widely advertised as a response to the need for 'facilities to be provided which are properly and professionally controlled for the benefit of the patient'. Fees for each surgical procedures are graded and Sister Rose also provides beauty treatment and dietary control.

All clinics warn patients of the need to understand fully what is involved but it is rarely suggested that cosmetic surgery may not help you to look younger and feel happier. In the words of Park Clinic's brochure, 'although we cannot stop the clock we can turn it back a little'. The Grahame Allen brochure from Manchester also explicitly draws attention to the fact that although 'some of the illustrations portray women, it goes without saying that all procedures, with obvious exceptions, apply equally well to men and women!'

134

The youth-enhancing properties of cosmetic surgery are best illustrated by the following story. A 50-year-old man married a girl of 20 claiming he was 10 years younger. After fourteen years of marriage the wrinkles began to show and his wife, who still found his body young, but his face old, said he looked like an old-aged pensioner. When he finally admitted his age his wife told him it would be a good idea if his face matched his body, and he decided to have a face lift to save his marriage. Two months later his wife, aged thirty-five, let him make love to her: 'When I saw his new face I was completely overwhelmed. I wanted to make love to him there and then and we did and it was wonderful. Our marriage is now complete and we are making love at least four times a day.' His true age was discovered when he became a pensioner at the age of 65. 'The new face has changed my life. I am buying new clothes and I feel even fitter now that I look the age that I've always pretended to be.'

If exercise, diet and cosmetic surgery fail or do not appeal we can still turn to the corsetry trade for support. Although the supportive function of corsetry has by no means been entirely replaced, advertisements now tend to concentrate on appearance rather than health. Thus the 'Bodymould' offers total figure support from under the bust right down to the thighs where it eliminates unsightly bulges completely, and gives the wearer the chance to put on 'close-fitting clothes you didn't dream possible'. In a line drawing it is shown worn beneath tight-fitting jeans. Another firm offers 'Slim Looks at a Low Price: Combining excellent control and elegant comfort with real economy.' (Ten months' free credit.) The new stretch fabrics have brought the possibility of doing without too many unsightly extra bulges underneath clothing; the 'front-loading bra' which came out in 1979 is an example. Another innovation, 'New super smooth, lightweight pantees in figure hugging Lycra, that show off your trousers, not themselves. White, Honey or Black', is also designed to give a natural finish. 'Don't let what you wear underneath spoil what you wear on top: Be some body in Silhouette Undi-tectables.' And whilst the one-piece corset still lives it too is now made from more flexible fabrics which in the adverts look almost like a second skin.

Yet even here the 'naturally' youthful body has triumphed. Within the space of a few decades the dominant mood has occasioned a shift from heavy-duty corsetry through to 'foundation garments', and now 'bodygarments' whose function is less to constrain and support excess flesh than to frame a firm and flexible physique. The concept of youth, fitness and beauty finds favour among women whose efforts to reduce the weight of age are displayed in new styles of undress. The freedom of the younger image is expressed in trimmed down flesh and supportive musculature. Women *are* generally fitter and the new stretch fabrics demand sleeker lines. On the corset market there is a 'new respect for the body' shared, of course, by men, some of whom have, since the late 1960s, appeared in advertisements for female underwear. The fashion for jeans is only one of the most obvious changes making the elimination of the matronly image of corsetry even more essential.

9

New Sex Lives for Old

In the imagery of the new middle age, sexual experimentation is never far away. One woman recently explained how she had reinvigorated her sex life after forty by replacing her 'dreary work-a-day clothing' with young clothes — smart slacks, shorter skirts and outfits which revealed her figure. Before this transformation she had worn an apron even when watching TV. She also, said her husband, bought alluring undies, which made him put aside his bedtime books and pay her more attention: 'I even got to look forward to bed.'

This person is by no means alone in defining the middle years as an appropriate time for sexual revitalization. A letter published by Claire Rayner typically observes:

My husband and I have been married for nearly ten years and have two lovely daughters. Basically our marriage has been good, but now our problem is sex. Over the years our sex life has dwindled. We've reached the stage where each of us knows every move the other will make and there is no thrill any more. Now he says he would like to go with another woman — not for life, but satisfaction and the thrill of somebody different. He says he loves me and doesn't want to hurt me and that it would only be a physical thing with somebody else. I don't want to lose my husband. I love him deeply and want our marriage to be a good one.

This lady was advised:

If he's telling you he wants another woman, and not another person, the remedy is simple — become the other woman yourself! . . . Ask your husband to teach you what he wants from you. He knows what would make him feel more needed and loved and less frustrated. Try to get someone to look after the children for the weekend, for example, and go off to a quiet hotel and spend all the time in bed. Read all the useful sex information books you can (I'm sending you a list of some you can buy by post) and set out to find your own hidden potential as an exciting lover.

In their popular manual *Treat Yourself to Sex*, sex therapists Paul Brown and Carolyn Faulder show how chronological age is far less detrimental to pleasurable sexual potency than boredom:

We strongly suspect that sheer tedium, a feeling of 'I've done all this a million times and I'm fed up' is behind much middle-aged impotence. . . . If a couple who have been together for many years no longer find any joy or delight in their sex life, then they must decide for themselves whether they are going to try to revitalise it.

Their recipe for the revitalization of mid-life sex includes a number of 'sexpieces' which begin with solitary relaxation and the scrutiny of one's naked body in the mirror, continue with the exploration of one's own body, and end with a partner with whom intercourse does not take place until a number of stages including mutual massage with body lotion have been completed. A couple, they say:

> May well find that it is when their family has grown up and left home and the struggles and pre-occupations of the first twenty-odd years are behind them, that the time is ripe for a profound reevaluation of their whole relationship, including its sexual aspects. If they continue to care for one another, they may reap long-term dividends by making a real investment in renewing the quality of their sex life.

In place of the traditional idea that sexual appetite naturally wanes with the onset of middle age and sex may therefore become less urgent or exciting, there is now a preoccupation with methods of renewing 'that loving feeling' or how to stop 'taking each other for granted'; in other words, in coping with the changes in physical attraction and intimate relations the passage of time can bring. Thus *The Complete Book of Sexual Love* is exuberantly advertised as a guide to methods of prolonging sexual excitement from adolescence to the grave. Dedicated to the principle that 'sex can be *infinitely* varied, *infinitely* exciting and *infinitely* NEW' throughout every period of married life, the aim of this manual is to show 'how the excitement of a couple's first encounters together can be made to last a whole life long. From the honeymoon to the Golden Anniversary and beyond.'

And in this context new heroes and heroines of mid-life sex have appeared: 'Are Jenni and Toni Mould Britain's Sexiest Couple? They make love 28 times a week at their home in Tooting, South London, and more when they are on holiday.' In their mid thirties and both into their fourth marriage they are an ecstatic and energetic example of how one couple has been able to revitalize a stagnant sex life.

Such prodigious performances in middle age are of course unusual. But sex advice for the middle aged now takes into account all sorts and conditions: the respectably married (those who wish to stay married to the same person but who feel that their sex lives have become rather routinized); unmarried or widowed men and women; and also the ever-expanding band of swingers and swappers who may well be married but are also interested in sexual experimentation that does not lead to the divorce courts. There is abundant evidence, therefore, that sexual expectations of the middle aged are gradually changing. Marriage guidance counsellors and sex therapists now describe sex as a developing capacity in which experimentation and fantasy play an important part in enlarging sexual tastes as one gets older or becomes 'mature'. The extension of the plateau of middle age and the increasing acceptance of sex in old age is creating a freer zone and an interest in performance and satisfaction.

Sex therapist Paul Brown told *The Sun* readers that 'after the early excitement of being married many couples lose the simple pleasures of being touched'. Modern marriage guidance counsellors encourage couples to spend a few hours a week discovering the sensations they may have lost. Another expert observes:

Sex can become a terrible barrier in a relationship because a couple imagine everyone else but them is having a marvellous time in bed. So when we persuade a couple to spend time alone together we ban sex until further notice, so that the pressure of having to make love isn't there.

Instead they have to touch, massage and explore each other's bodies.

The effects, says Paul Brown, are often extraordinary:

Many illnesses caused by tension, such as headaches and backaches, disappear completely. Most people are miserable if they don't have a good relationship. Yet they do nothing to value and maintain it. Touch makes you close to someone and that's what a relationship is all about.

According to this approach, sex is no longer simply a means of procreation and the expression of affection within the sanctity of marriage but also a method of toning up the body, reducing the chances of ill-health, combating obesity, developing sensual awareness and extending or renewing the personality. Like jogging, enhanced sexual performance allegedly opens up new horizons on each of which is visible an ever-expanding range of benefits.

Turning on to sex means turning on to life. When your sexy senses are awakened you will find heightened pleasure all around you — not just in the bedroom. The world will look more beautiful. You will appreciate good food more, you will find yourself listening to the music coming out of your

141

radio, you will notice the crisp smell of apples outside the grocers. And you can turn the turn-ons round. You do not need to fall in love to stimulate your sexy senses. Try waking up to the smells, sounds and sights around you and you will find yourself waking up to the tingling touch of sexual pleasure.

An important prerequisite for the enjoyment of this new sexualized life to the full is physical fitness: the assumption being that physical fitness breeds confidence in the body and the ability to use it more energetically in love-making, which, since it should be prolonged, now requires greater stamina.

Perhaps the fullest description of this emerging world of sexuality can be found in Gay Talese's book *Thy Neighbour's Wife*, a number one bestseller in the United States, where it grossed $4 million in pre-publication rights alone. Described as 'a trim tennis-playing 48 year old', Talese set out on an eight-year investigation of the 'hidden sexual world that lurked beneath the surface of America's respectable middle aged'. During this odyssey he managed a massage parlour called the Secret Life where he discovered most of the customers were middle class and middle aged. 'They were enjoying half an hour with a young body. It was as if the centrefold of *Playboy* magazine had suddenly come to life and walked towards them.' Talese believes the sexual revolution in the 1980s is going to involve an emphasis on pleasure, and one new feature of this is the fact that women are increasingly falling under the influence of this idea and becoming more sexually demanding. If, however, they are going to get their share of sexual action, middle-aged men and women must be in good condition, primed, as it were, for the casual sexual encounter. As Talese observed in an interview in *The Sun* in May 1980:

Healthy fit people are more sexual. The emphasis on keeping in condition, looking well, being firm of muscle, sinewy, with a flat stomach and good legs is all part of the game of attracting the opposite sex. Good health and good sex are compatible.

On 16 June 1980, Marje Proops explained the implications of Gay Talese's book to her readers:

The other day I replied to a letter I'd had from a suburban housewife who asked if I would advise husband-swapping as an effective way of improving a humdrum marriage. The letter came as no surprise to me. Yet twenty years ago I would have been amazed to receive it.

Despite awful warnings, about what another popular daily newspaper described as 'Wife Swap Peril!', there is no evidence that swinging and swapping is decreasing in popularity, although for it to operate as a successful underground activity it has to be carefully organized, staged, and the roles of the various participants clearly laid down in advance. In what has been described by one writer as the 'velvet underground', discretion is the watchword. Other key qualities are sincerity, cleanliness, 'genuineness' and an endless capacity for 'fun' and 'friendliness'. In the more academic literature, sociologists have tended to use the terms 'mate swapping', 'spouse swapping', 'swinging', 'co-marital sex', and 'group sex' to refer to the willingness of married couples to exchange partners and engage in sexual activities with other couples. Intimate contact usually takes place between exchanged partners at the same time and place. This may involve participants moving into separate rooms for 'closed swinging' or joining in communal or 'open swinging' — a swingers' party, where three or more partners engage in group sex, while others watch.

Whatever other sexual preferences they may reveal, the increasing number of intriguing personal ads in contact magazines testify to the fact that many swingers and swappers are men and women in early middle age:

'Plump, 33 year old housewife 42 inch breasts has husband's approval to meet men, 30—35 years, daytime or evening for sex'; 'Sexy couple, late-30s, she AC/DC'; 'Couple, early 40s both well-built'; 'Dominant lady, late-30s'; 'Genuine attractive couple, married, both in early 30s'; 'Happily married couple, 40s, would like to meet other genuine swingers'; 'Over sexed 38-year-old woman 38, 28, 38 happily married, with husband's approval, seeks men friends'; 'Uninhibited couple, but discreet and genuine, he 52, vasectomised, she 46, sexy. Seek mature couples for sexual pleasures, swapping, foursomes, parties'; 'Attractive couple, both 40, seek long-term friendship with like couple, swapping if compatible. Sensitive couples with reasonable standard of living only'; 'Gent, semi-retired, 58, seeks lady, 45—60, for sex fun.'

It would, of course, be foolish to suggest that all swingers are middle aged but it is certainly the case that there is, under the flag of convenience of the new sexuality, a place for 'broad-minded adults'. One way of revitalizing the humdrum marital relationship

144

is to ring the changes within the carefully organized and discreet contexts of swinging and swapping. Contact with partners through the medium of magazine advertisements takes place under a cloak of respectability which mail order firms for contraceptives, exotic glamour wear, 'marital aids', and sex toys also find profitable. It is nowadays more possible than before for people to move between two worlds which have their own rules and boundaries. Within the private world of modern sexuality, exotic practices and seductive fantasy have become commonplace, and the signs are that many are casting more than a speculative eye in this direction.

What, then, are the most outstanding features of this new experimental world of sexuality? Firstly, the belief in sex as a skilled physical performance which should give greater and greater satisfactions if it is carefully rehearsed. Sex manuals now describe in precise detail the techniques necessary to achieve 'The Secret Joys of Sexual Fulfilment', 'The Ectasy of Sex', and of pursuing, for example, 'Adventures in Oral Sex', or getting the most out of 'Exotic Love Games'. The notion that sex can be the highest expression of romantic attachment and affection is complicated by the contemporary notion that sex is really a form of work for which technical knowledge is essential to achieve the maximum satisfaction now believed to be a fundamental human right. Couples are urged to adopt an instrumental approach to the sex act and judge each performance by the amount of physical pleasure it produces. Because physical fitness is an important factor the emphasis is inevitably upon the attributes of youthfulness: physical fitness, athleticism, energy, stamina and power.

The second feature of modern sexual experimentation is the encouragement of erotic fantasy. Marriage guidance counsellors, sex therapists and even agony aunties now openly advise men and women to pursue their sexual fantasies. In 1979 Claire Rayner published this letter in *The Sun*:

> I am so mixed up. I am 32 and my husband is 33. We have been married for 8 years. My problem is sex. We love each other very much and our only regular argument is because he makes requests for unusual sex, like me dressing up and pretending games. I have done it a few times and hated it.

And the advice:

> There is nothing odd about sharing sexy games. It's time you stopped fighting over sex and started to talk about your real feelings.

An earlier letter, again to Claire Rayner, from a troubled wife, had run:

> Today I came home earlier than expected and found a 'Girlie' publication my husband had been reading and obviously forgotten to hide. I was shocked and hurt, that he felt the need for something I can only describe as disgusting.

She was advised to calm down. At least she hadn't found her husband in the arms of another woman:

> Just a set of glossy pages. Why did he do it? Bless you because he's a normal fellow with normal interests and appetites. These publications give men a giggle, a mild erotic thrill, and perhaps a

few ideas for improving their love making when they are with the real woman they love.

The most explicit examples of sexual fantasy occur, of course, in specialized porn where 'Nympho Nurses', 'Schoolgirl Dreams', 'Nude Wives', 'The Ultimate Orgasm', and a host of peeping plumbers, insatiable nuns and other lusty characters can be found. Much closer to respectable everyday life, however, is the constant stream of small ads in popular and quality newspapers for catalogues of 'glamourwear' and 'fantasy fashions'.

Here the range is from conventional 'leisurewear' to what are usually described as 'sexy', 'risqué', 'sensational', or 'erotic' sets: glamourwear which 'will more than cater for your every fantasy'. These items are designed to ring the changes on a limited number of body-packaging themes: the framing of breasts, belly, buttocks, genitals and thighs. Nipples are exposed in cut-out bras and the vulva in crotchless knickers. 'Sensational see-through nighties' from which the breasts protrude induce 'giddy intoxication'. Satin Basques 'will shape curve and transform you into the sexiest of shapes', giving the promise of 'everything a man ever wanted'. Sensual nightwear allows 'the "Secret You" to be unveiled'. Other combinations can 'Give your charms that extra lift and reach the highest star in the heavens with Zenith — the ultimate in revealing playsuits' -- in slinky black wet look with 'open-crotch' feature. The ever popular suspender belt can be worn in combination with a G-string and the quarter cup bra offers 'complete freedom' being in effect merely a support for the almost naked breasts and fully exposed nipples.

Such is the popularity of body packaging that the

more sedate mail order firms which cater for all the family are now offering a modest line in basques (Berlei Gypsy Basque) and suspender belts amongst their stocks of conventional bras, pantee girdles, and pantee corselets. They also offer a line in nylon, satin and lace-trimmed lingerie. This trade was supported in *The News of the World* women's column of 16 November 1980, where male readers were encouraged to buy undies 'as a surprise present for the women in your life. There is no need to be shy. Lingerie shop assistants will do everything they can to make you feel at ease.' Thus encouraged, men are openly buying lingerie as a present for their wives and Christmastime now brings what was described in one quality Sunday newspaper as the 'lingerie harvest'.

One of *The Sun*'s not infrequent surveys on 'sex and love in the 1980s' revealed that an important arousal factor was 'wearing specially sexy clothes, like black lace underwear or lots of leather. Thirty-one per cent of men and women get a thrill out of dressing for sex.' A quarter of the men in the survey were turned on 'by the idea of sex aids, like vibrators, which only appeal to one in seven women'. Mirrors and cameras add a dash of excitement for one in five men and one in eight women 'who like to reflect on their own loving images'. Alas, dressing up for sex can have unforseen consequences. It was reported not long ago that a man who got his kicks from seeing his mistress clad in black stockings and a frilly lace suspender belt could not contain his anger when she put them on and went to a dance without him.

An indication of the popularity of these intimate items can be found in the offer made by one large glamourwear mail order firm of 'The Wash-In-One-

148

Bag', a zip-up nylon mesh bag with a tough corrosion resistant zip which has apparently been a success in America for over 20 years. Into this you put your various items of intimate glamourwear to take to the launderette where they are concealed from the prying eyes of other patrons who may not share your taste in risqué clothing. The garments can thus be washed with complete confidence, privately, in public. The high-quality leaflet advertising this particular item shows a trim, carefully groomed middle-aged woman, the lines on whose face are skilfully covered with make-up, transfixed in the act of transferring a 'Wash in One Bag' filled with unidentifiable items into her washing machine.

One of the declared aims of merchandisers is to overcome the boredom of routinized sex stemming from familiarity with the same partner over a number of years. Each garment is set against a background of sensual comfort and warmth. All women look seductive: 'Drive him bananas in this sensational topless, open-crotch, backless playsuit'; 'Romp around the bedroom in this saucy open-crotch playsuit with naughty cut-away sides and lace-trim'; 'Get your man every time in this exciting backless one-piece playsuit.' Although the models are usually youthful, many size charts are divided into small, medium and extra large, offering something in fact for everybody. And now and again there is a representation of a trim, harmonious middle-aged couple. Husband and wife, for example, are caught in the act of opening a brown paper parcel, she taking out a folded basque and looking invitingly at the camera, while he, hand on hip, smilingly inclines his head towards her in obvious approval. The implication is that the happy pair have just got their hands on the prospect of even greater marital harmony and bliss; the good times have only just begun.

Whilst the majority of items are clearly designed to have a 'devastating', 'unusual', or 'sophisticated' impact on the male, flimsy sex wear for men is creeping in. An expanding range of briefs and G-strings modelled by youthful men, whose generative equipment is teasingly confined in wet-look pouches, or denim and Tanga briefs (all garments come in small, medium, large and extra large sizes) is now available.

The link-up between body packaging and sexual experimentation in the privacy of one's own home is made even more explicit in certain glamourwear catalogues by the inclusion of coupons which can be sent away for catalogues of marital aids and sex toys. Here the advertisements are for films, books and equipment, the express aim of which is to extend physical sensations and reinforce sexual fantasies:

> As society becomes more enlightened towards sexual problems, and aware that so many present day problems stem for sexual frustration, the benefits of sexual aids to promote fulfilment are unquestionable. This catalogue has been designed in an attempt to re-invigorate, and possibly stimulate, marital relationships.

Because these goods are designed to stimulate and increase sexual appetite, a substantial number have the capacity to appeal either implicitly or explicitly to the apparently flagging appetites of the older consumer. Alongside the inflatable dolls, plastic organs, rubberwear, leatherwear ('Tasty Pants: Wear it — then eat it. In delicious cherry flavour with liquorice ties'), considerable space is devoted to allegedly invigorating creams, potions, pills and jellies:

Red Stallion Capsules — Iron hooves pounding the rugged turf, sleek iron muscles powering their way forward, a red stallion surges out of the mist.

And:

Black Tiger Capsules — Streamlined power behind the rippling, taut, black surface, every fibre poised to spring, the black tiger pounces.

Then there is:

Instant Firming Oil — If it's already hard but you could stand it even harder, or if you'd like to give it a little help getting big and hard just 'one more time'.

'Mr Big' erection cream and 'Female Bliss Cream' have also been designed to pleasure the demanding female whose partner should, however, be informed of the dangers:

Comfort Oil is the answer for those sore genitals that using Mr Big, or Prolong, or Spurious Spanish Fly can happily create. After you've done all the wonderfully pleasing damage that you can do to a girl show her how gentle and caring you can be by taking care of her sorely abused love channels.

A wide variety of tonic products are marketed to tone up the middle aged: 'Another male tonic and supplement stronger than Testrones, containing extra gland and vital principles. It is a favourite with middle aged men and has world-wide acclaim.' And for women: 'A female tonic supplement specially recommended for middle aged women, for many years Overones have enjoyed acclaim for enabling women to enjoy a more active life.' Breast developers and bust creams mingle with erection aids, padded sheathes, penile supports and penis developers with mind-boggling properties. An astonishing variety of dildos is, for example, designed among other things, 'to assist couples in maintaining the physical side of their marriages if (by injury, temporary impotency, or other reasons) harmonious sexual relationships are virtually impossible'. One line of erect plastic male genitals is itemized as 'Sexual Prosthetics (Artificial Organs)', with the assurance they closely resemble 'the complete male genitals in form, texture and elasticity'.

As far as the general population of middle-aged men and women is concerned the expanding realm of sexual experimentation operates on a variety of levels. It is most completely realized in the world discovered in the States by Gay Talese during the course of his sexual investigations for *Thy Neighbour's Wife*. Famous exponents of the swinging lifestyle include Hugh Heffner, inventor of the *Playboy* fantasy and Bob Guccione, publisher of *Penthouse*. These men are totally dedicated to the delights of the youthful body, surviving on their skill in marketing fantasies on a scale hitherto unprecedented. Whether or not these fantasies can ever be realized amidst the humdrum routine of everyday life is less important for most of us than the dream of sexual adventure and even of self-realization they purvey. To some extent all of us in middle age are consumers of this dream, which is an important facet of the new image of middle age. Perhaps the final comment should come from Ronald Dawson, publisher of several sex contact magazines, who placed an advert in a national sex magazine inviting couples to make a colour and sound videotape of their lovemaking:

Many folk like to see themselves making love, but until now the only way has been to produce a home movie. Often the results aren't very good. We think it best to shoot the action in video. Customers get an instant replay and mistakes can be put right. To try to make things really interesting we work out some sort of script for the couple beforehand — give the thing a storyline like TV. Apart from the cameraman it's a private and personal business. And the customer has the only copy of the film. We're sure it will give a lot of happy memories. Who knows, couples might want to look at themselves in later years when all the passion has gone.

Thanks to mid-life sex, passion need not yet fade — at least for those with the will and the way to prolong their active lives.

10

New Identities for Old

If anyone has any doubts about the new lease of life middle age can bring, he or she need only turn to Bernice and Morton Hunt for exuberant reassurance. Middle age, they claim in their book *Prime Time*, has at last emerged as one of the best periods of our life, a period which contrasts sharply with the earlier dreary stereotypes: women who, having led active lives as housewives and mothers till forty, had little choice but to accept the role loss and loneliness of the years of the 'empty nest'. Middle-aged husbands too had lost their fire and readily fell asleep in the chair after dinner, yet despite their greying hair and paunchy stomachs, their wives lived in constant fear that their husbands would go chasing off after younger women. The Hunts assert that the real-life counterpart of this traditional image is getting harder and harder to find. In its place are middle-aged men and women who are taking a much more positive attitude to life and consequently enjoy greater bodily and psychological health. As the Hunts put it:

Thanks to recent research which has made us aware of the life-saving value of proper diet and adequate exercise, most middle-aged men and women are

154

trimmer and more physically active than their predecessors.

Middle-aged people today are still physically young and what is more they think young. Married couples have more time and money to enjoy better sex and deeper intimacy and to explore their personal identities:

For the first time since their own childhood parents can be largely inner-directed, employing their newly released time and energy to develop the ego-pleasing and ego-satisfying facets of their own personalities.

Norman and Gina O'Neill also follow this approach in their book *Shifting Gears* where they attack 'the maturity myth'. This myth, they say, rests on the dangerous and false belief that we should strive to achieve our external goals by forty, after which we will be 'home and safe', the active side of life completed — and thence downhill all the rest of the way, a deplorable approach to the passing years:

The tendency to resignation or defeat is encouraged by false ideas about what happens to our physical, mental and sexual vitality from the forties on. Our society has begun to get away from the belief that pot bellies, sagging jowls, flabby skin, and physical inertia naturally and inevitably come with age — and maturity. Physical fitness exercises of one sort or another have gained a new popularity in recent years; we don't always undertake them for the right reasons, but at least we are moving in the right direction. Even so, we have got rid of the idea that a degree of mental capacity is lost as we age. The fact is, according to recent research, that physical exercise can actually improve our mental capacities.

With the right attitude then, ageing need not mean physical, mental and sexual decline. 'We don't stop growing ever', they tell us, and applaud the lawyer who said:

For me middle age is sixty-five or over, if you have to call it that. From age thirty, and I'll be there in two days, to aged sixty-five is really middle Youth.

For the O'Neills and many similar writers, middle age is a time for active self-exploration. Uncomfortable experiences such as the mid-life crisis are to be welcomed since they are perfectly normal transitions which offer a new chance of growth and fulfilment. If we face up to and create our own challenges, we will discover new resources and competences. Because we live in what is often described as a 'crisis culture', where the old supports and values have broken down, we need to take risks and develop a strong sense of self with firm commitments.

The injunction to 'self actualize' is found in another popular treatment *The Wonderful Crisis of Middle Age* by Eda Le Shan. Here the mid-life crisis is seen to present 'the greatest opportunity one has ever had to become most truly alive and ourself'. It offers the chance of continuing our adolescent identity crisis; a second chance to find out what it really means to 'do your own thing' and to be 'deeply truly yourself'. Perhaps, as we mentioned earlier, the

156

best known book of this type is Gail Sheehy's *Passages*. Putting forward a variant of the 'life as an obstacle course' theme, Sheehy argues that all men and women experience predictable crisis every seven years, and these are a necessary part of the process of maturation. After our 'creative mid-life crises' we can look forward to a middle age in which we develop new interests, hobbies, and keep busy in an apparently unlimited process of self-development:

> If I've been convinced by one idea in the course of collecting all the life stories that inform the book it is this: Times of crisis, of disruption or constructive change, are not only predictable but desirable. They mean growth.

The pattern then is set out for us. Whether or not we succeed depends upon our effort and capacity to let the old self die and allow the new to grow.

That there is an expanding market for advocates of self-exploration and methods of its attainment is reflected in the late 1970s estimate that one in five Americans have taken up some form of therapy, ranging from consultations with a psychiatrist through to joining a consciousness-raising group, where the aim is to improve self understanding. There is evidence too that interest has spread to Britain where an increasing preoccupation with self-exploration and self-development, especially amongst people beyond the first flush of youth, can readily be found. Books like Eric Berne's *Games People Play*, one of the basic texts of transactional analysis, and Frederick S. Perls's *In and Out of the Garbage Pail* have easily adapted to the British market. Another bestseller, J. Greenwald's *Be the Person You Want to Be*, asserts:

Awareness is an endlessly available opportunity offering the possibilities of new discoveries of who one is and who one isn't. The limitless potential to experience the joy and excitement of learning about oneself and one's world can make life a meaningful adventure for anyone.

One interesting personality who has published his personal voyage of self-discovery through these various self-awareness groups is Jerry Rubin, who was in early middle age when he first felt the need to change his way of life. In the late 1960s he was author of *Do It*, the Yippee Manifesto, a radical appeal to the youth of the day. In his subsequent autobiography he observes:

One day in December, 1974, I was eating pitta bread and in a restaurant in the West Village with some friends, Lennie Weinglass looked up and asked me, 'Do you think there is such a thing as a *male* menopause? . . . In the 1960s I would have laughed at the idea of male menopause, but now my mind ticked off all my male friends in their thirties. A few continued with enthusiasm, but many were experiencing the common symptoms of depression, low energy, and loss of ambition. What had caused it? The ageing process?

Rubin's salvation was conversion to the pursuit of self-actualization:

In five years, from 1971 to 1975, I directly experienced est (Erhardt Seminar Training), gestalt therapy, bioenergetics, rolfing, massage, jogging, health foods, tai chi, Esalen, hypnotism, modern dance, meditation, Silva Mind Control, Arica, acupuncture, sex therapy, Reichian therapy, and More House — a smorgasbord course in New Consciousness.

After years of neglect he began to look after his body, shed 30 lb and 'felt at 37 like 25'. He got rid of his 'puritan conditioning' and 'learned to love myself enough that I do not need another to make me happy'. These emergent narcissistic tendencies blend neatly with the youth, fitness and beauty emphasis on 'looking good' which encourages us to make the most of our appearance, to conserve the body as well as the self because it is all we possess and we must needs enjoy it as long as possible.

Jerry Rubin's personality change accompanied his change of address from New York to California. And it is in California that beautiful people with lithe tanned bodies and relaxed smiles reflect the 'I've seen the future and it works' view lingering behind much of the youth, fitness and beauty media imagery of middle age. This imagery has its attractions, especially to those of us who have been brought up according to stricter codes emphasizing the value of duty, diligence, hard work, and repressed feelings, and who thus now feel entitled to some rewards after the sacrifices that have been made for family and career. The imagery holds out the promise of more exciting relationships as long, of course, that physical attractiveness has been preserved.

The new middle age depends on a flexible conception of both body and personality: you are what you make yourself and the goal of life is to understand oneself and construct a satisfactory identity. Instead of adulthood being regarded as a complete stage of personality development, the popular self-help literature presents middle age as a phase of life where crises and painful reassessment can lead to regeneration and positive growth.

Amongst their case histories the Hunts include an aeronautics engineer in California who moved to a ski lodge in Colorado, a construction boss who set himself up to run a summer vacation camp, and a doctor who became a freelance writer. Such cases are drawn from the higher reaches of the middle class to confirm the thesis that self-help really works, but there is also the more interesting implication that for every individual who actually takes a decisive step to change his life in middle age there are many others who experience similar discontents and do nothing about it. Our own research on middle-aged persons who go missing in Britain suggests that while some individuals go missing in search of identity change, many others with similar desires remain at home and put up with personal dissatisfaction. In this situation the person who strikes out to resolve his mid-life crisis is often accorded the admiration of his peers. Nancy Mayer tells of a 45-year-old vice-president of a publishing house who gave up his job to devote himself to writing his autobiography. He was surprised by the envy he aroused:

The curious thing was the number of men who came up to me: surgeons, lawyers, advertising men, men who were making much more money than I was, averaging $150,000 a year, and who had magnificent oceanfront houses. Out of 200 families there, I must know 100 men well enough to talk to. And that summer I don't think there was a man under 50 who didn't stop me. The conversation usually centred on 'How did you have enough guts to do it?'

Several decades before the Hunts and other writers described cases of dramatic personal change in mid life, the literary mould had been cast by Somerset Maugham in his novel *The Moon and Sixpence*, probably his best known work. The inspiration for the story of Charles Strickland was the life of the artist Paul Gauguin. Strickland is a boringly respectable middle-aged stockbroker who, to everyone's astonishment, suddenly abandons his family and goes to Paris. The narrator, a younger man and friend of the family, is persuaded to pursue him for an explanation. He discovers that Strickland has not, as everyone at home imagines, run off with a tea-shop girl:

'I want to paint.' I looked at him for a long time. I did not understand. I thought he was mad. It must be remembered that I was very young, and I looked upon him as a middle-aged man. I forgot everything but my own amazement. 'But you're forty.' 'That's what made me think it was high time to begin.'

The Gauguin *Moon and Sixpence* theme harnesses a powerful undercurrent in our culture: the desire for personal change that will allow authentic self-expression — often popularly labelled 'doing a Gauguin'. Perhaps of all Maugham's themes, says Ted Morgan, the most recent biographer, that of 'the world well lost is the most persistent':

Many were the Sunday painters reading *The Moon and Sixpence* who thought to themselves pourquoi

161

pas moi. . . . There is one recorded case of a highly successful individual who really did chuck it all up at over fifty to go to the South Seas and paint as a result of reading Maugham. This was the American Ray Long, the editor of Cosmopolitan Magazine. . . . Unfortunately Long's efforts as a painter were not crowned with success and he died by his own hand.

In more recent times the market has seized upon the notion of 'doing a Gauguin' and painless versions are now available. Thus on 3 October 1980, the *Mirror* reported:

Men are queueing for a new package holiday — three weeks in a China Sea coral island beach hut with a dusky maiden. Philippino women, said the charter pilot organising the trips, 'are naturally warm and loving'. Though not selling sex he confirmed there were plenty of beautiful girls 'who would jump at the chance of romance with a personable man'. The Association of British Travel Agents, however, was quick to point out 'Tour operators should not hold out romance as part of the deal.'

The problem, as Ray Long discovered to his cost, is that the myth is one thing and reality another. John Koffend, an associate editor of *Time* magazine, is another American who found complete personal change a more challenging task than he imagined. At the age of fifty-two, with a broken marriage behind him, he quit his job and headed out for the Polynesian island of Samoa. His account of his crisis, *A Letter to My Wife*, is a tortured, self-pitying document, a testament to the difficulty of finding oneself and confirmation that exotic surroundings do not always work their magic and deliver up the desired 'true self'. After his move to Polynesia he writes:

I've been here almost two months now. It's been a long day. I'm tired and awash with beer and my thoughts are as unsteady as my hand. Samoa, I've half decided, is not a solution or an escape route from whatever I was fleeing. . . . As in New York I stubbornly resist and resent facing the mirror. There he is, that middle aged man, showing his years plainly, pretending that he has somehow evaded their toll. I'm going to die, sooner than you, sooner than nearly everyone younger than I: and still persist in the self-deception that I don't look fifty-three and am not fifty-three and can slide under that accumulation of years to retrieve the lost time, beat the clock.

Here is the classic mid-life crisis obsession with mortality, wasted time, and a concern for lost youth and deteriorating appearance. Before his move, Koffend had been systematic and disciplined, rigidly adhering to a fitness schedule of 150 sit-ups, 50 press-ups, and 1,500 running-on-the-spot exercises a day, which he claimed 'is still pretty impressive for a man of my age and habits'. When questioned about his motives by a friend who caught him exercising in his office, he replied, 'to stay in shape' and when the friend persisted with his interrogation he could not answer. Later in the book he noted the difficulty of completing his sit-ups routine — 'I must be getting old' — then decided to do another set to prove he is still able.

The feeling that life has not kept its promise, that

there must be something more than boring daily routine, unfortunately does not always produce a creative mid-life crisis which leads to growth. The dreams we form in childhood and early adulthood may well be pure dreams or fantasies: completely out of reach in our existing world. Daniel Levinson, the American psychologist, has argued that the dreams of many working-class men are of this kind — fantasies of being a sports superstar or macho cowboy hero which gradually disintegrate amidst the day-to-day struggle for survival. As in the case of Koffend's ultimately fruitless journey, many of us possessed by vague feelings of unease, boredom and listlessness may face a mid-life crisis which will not crystallize, apparent escape serving only to intensify feelings of stagnation. This may be particularly true for women who have not traditionally been encouraged to form a dream or seek self-realization. Barbara Fried in *Middle Age Crisis* mentions a woman who ran away from her home and family and drove across America with a boy half her age. She returned after a month or so, and commented with bewildered resignation: 'It happened — I couldn't help myself. It was wonderful and I'm not sorry that I did it. But what good was it? It didn't change anything.'

The media, which help to give credibility to the image of middle age as a time of personal renewal, are also quick to seize on stories of victims and casualties. There are, it seems, many successful people who find the glamorous lifestyle ultimately only amounts to a shallow world of 'users' who long for, but are incapable of finding, 'deep meaningful relationships'. The quest for 'true love' has been a prominent theme in the recent spate of popular Hollywood and Californian novels. Joyce Haber's bestseller, *The Users*, describes

how Elena Brent, one of Hollywood's most successful hostesses, finds herself struggling desperately not
to fall in love with Adam Baker. He is a younger man
on the make whom she suspects has coolly singled
her out as a passport to the smart set and a movie
career. Despite her doubts, she finally decides to
sacrifice the security of her luxurious lifestyle for the
meaningful and loving relationships she hopes he
really holds out, only to have her fears that he has
been merely using her confirmed.

In *Sunday Simmons and Charlie Brick*, Jackie
Collins moves to and fro between detailed descriptions of the Hollywood beautiful people and a mean,
grubby lower-class film studio chauffeur who plots
perverse 'revenge' sex fantasies on the stars. His fat,
lazy wife perpetually stuffs herself with food while
she watches TV all day. The central character, Charlie
Brick, a former small-time English comic, is now an
international star exposed to the Hollywood lifestyle
yet obsessed with the emptiness of his marriage to a
young starlet and the futility of his middle-aged
efforts to stay young and attractive. He still longs for
his drab ex-wife who alone could provide the meaningful relationship he craved:

Why did people rest so much importance on
physical attributes? He did so himself. That was
why he dieted so strenuously and only took out
dozy starlets and models, and finally married one.
The lovely Dindi, who had absolutely nothing to
offer except her looks. Perhaps that was why he
still wanted Lorna, because she was an ordinary
person who had known him when he was a nobody.
He didn't fancy her, there was nothing sexual left,
but he still wanted her.

165

Even those Hollywood stars whose lives seem filled with the promise of the imagery still question the meaning of life. Indeed, the beauty salons of the stars very often include philosophical and spiritual guidance programmes which are not available in cheaper high street imitations. Many Hollywood stars spend years under costly psychoanalysis and attribute their success to the self-knowledge they have derived from it.

That such self-knowledge is a crucial element is further confirmed by a middle-aged Hollywood cosmetic surgeon and his wife interviewed by Alan Whicker in April 1980. Referring to the operations for chin implant, breast surgery and pinned-back ears which her husband had performed on her, she said she felt far less insecure than before: 'Kirk will never divorce me because he can always change me.' On closer questioning the surgeon himself revealed he had been through a critical period at forty when he questioned 'what it was all about, accomplishments, goals and aims' and found that psychoanalysis and 'est' had helped him through. His wife endorsed the psychological benefits of 'est' therapy and added that together cosmetic surgery and 'est' gave her 'fabulous confidence which no power on earth could take away'. Testimony to the potency of this combination of the body beautiful and self-exploration also comes from the inhabitants of America's self-proclaimed 'laboratory for the future', Marin County California. Anthea Disney reports that amongst this affluent white middle-class community of young and middle-aged people across the bay from San Francisco the social code is 'to get into your own mind and your own body, forget conventional morality, assume that instant gratification is desirable and above all be mellow'. Being mellow, or 'laid-back' involves joining the Human Potential Movement (the second most important industry of Marin County) and keeping fit. Marinites jog, swim, hike, bike and massage each other. A therapist explained the up-date of the Victorian 'healthy mind in a healthy body' message:

> Unless your body is in good shape, once the insides are coming through because you've worked on your mind, it's like putting 2,000 volts through a 1,000 volt socket. So automatically without knowing why, people who are involved in expanding their own consciousness start dealing with the body.

The earliest form the self-awareness movement took was the encounter group where members were encouraged to be open and honest. Encounter groups ostensibly offered situations where feelings could be expressed without fear of rejection and participants could learn to be in touch with their essential selves and so thus readjust positively to the world outside. But the changes which participation in encounter groups, est, yoga, and others, produce are often problematic in themselves because like swinging and swapping, they take place in special settings amongst selected participants whose conduct is regulated by specific rules. Participation, for example, in a weekend of consciousness-raising Primal Therapy is inevitably followed by a return to the conventional world although, of course, the participant may feel different inside. A further problem not unconnected with the wider world is the financial cost of participating in these various groups, many of which are provided by commercial organizations, as in the case of the multimillion doller est corporation.

167

The est method, a fictionalized version of which appeared in the BBC television play, *Instant Enlightenment Plus VAT*, is to isolate participants in a hotel room for something like 60 hours for a large fee. Est was founded in America by Werner Erhardt, a former used car salesman, who turned to the packaging of Mind Dynamics in the early 1970s. It is a fusion of encounter psychodrama, gestalt therapy, scientology, Zen Buddhism and Dale Carnegie. At the last estimate there were 100,000 graduates. Jerry Rubin described the training as follows:

> About two hundred people are packed into a hotel room on hard chairs for four eighteen hour days. Everyone agrees in advance not to eat, leave their seats, or talk unless called on. From the front of the room the trainer barrages people with an attack on their egos, roles and lifestyles, while at the same time giving academic lectures on the nature of reality, the meaning of life, and the process of perception. Then people go to the microphone to share from their hearts and souls the secrets they rarely tell their friends. At the end everyone is enlightened.

Taken in all its various manifestations, the awareness movement represents a commercialization of the desire of individuals for personal change in adult life which has emerged since the war. The emphasis is on pay-offs, the control of others, winning rather than losing, responsibility for the self, and the cultivation of a stronger ego.

As we have also noted, the awareness movement as a whole places great emphasis on the body and its secret strengths and limitations. Encounter groups

168

foster close links between blocked feelings and body work and some encounter techniques involve touching and exploring the body. Manuals on non-verbal communication (body language) also show us how to manipulate the body as a communication device. In other words, there are links with sex therapy and certain techniques of marriage guidance counselling and the general youth, fitness and beauty approach.

In their study *Snapping: America's Epidemic of Sudden Personality Change*, Conway and Siegelman refer to Jean Turner, who is described as a small, attractive, 52-year-old, college-educated mother of three, now divorced. She had read in a newspaper that her social status was categorized 'Displaced Homemaker':

> There are many of us and nobody has paid much attention to this group of women who, after years of raising children and husbands come to middle age and without a skill. What do you do then? You have no money, no security, nothing. What are you? I had raised my children through every kind of crisis imaginable. When they were grown up and healthy, I felt pretty good about it, but it was as though the most important part of my life was over. I had to find meaning. That's when I started the search.

She tried a four-day residential course of transcendental meditation where 'my mind and body were one'. She then joined an encounter group where her feelings of transcendence reached even higher: 'I just got high . . . it was a beautiful feeling of well-being, warmth and loving.' Transcendental meditation and the encounter group opened up to her new dimensions of experience. She then tried est and, following a negative emotional reaction, had a tremendous high, 'the most marvellous body feelings I've known'. She began to fantasize, lost touch with reality, began to speak in poetical language and was alone in her apartment for a week:

> I was getting a whole new body, a renewal. I was extremely active. I couldn't stop dancing. I didn't want to stop, it was too good. My body just felt so powerful.

Then the high toppled and she went sharply downwards and ended up in a psychiatric hospital on tranquillizers.

Another way of meeting someone who will help you to change your life (hopefully for the better) is through a singles club, friendship/marriage bureau, introduction consultant, contact and dating service or lonely hearts organization. One in four of Britain's adult population, it was announced in *The News of the World* in 1980, was a single person, and, we can add, a sizeable proportion of these are middle aged. A few decades ago the divorced and the widowed — and, of course, spinsters and bachelors who had not married when young — had to content themselves with relative isolation, splendid or otherwise. Now this is all changing. There are, as *The News of the World* was quick to point out, a growing number of respectable commercial organizations eager to help 'by letting the singles mingle'. At present introduction bureaux number between 60 and 100 and these are tailored to suit all pockets. They range from the up-market Prestige Partners (motto: 'people need people'), through Mastermatch to Consort Dating,

Jayne's Service, Kate's Introductions, and North of England Friendship Bureau. All provide the same basic service: an introduction to a person of the opposite sex who has been matched with varying degrees of precision to a client's personality profile. Inevitably the up-market agencies have the strongest recommendation: a lengthy list of lonely people who wish for introductions and therefore a greater likelihood of finding 'the right person for you'.

The London-based Prestige Partners (Introduction Consultants) Ltd advertise in *Tatler* and *Vogue* as 'The professional persons' friendship/marriage bureau'. Those who ring or write for details receive an imposing gold-embossed brochure addressed to the 'unattached professional, academic and business person'. The service covers the whole of England, Scotland, Wales and Ireland. There are franchised branches in Northern Ireland, Devon, Essex, Middlesex, Oxford and Liverpool. It has 'thousands of the right sort of people to call on' − more than 6,000 members who are chosen 'with extreme care', undesirables being weeded out by 'trained consultants'. Members are currently charged £86.25 and a marriage fee of £75. The basic service provides three names and phone numbers, following the completion of a detailed questionnaire which includes questions on the social class to which applicants ascribe themselves. The purpose of Prestige Partners is 'to introduce persons to each other with a view to friendship and/or marriage', to which end is offered the alluring prospect of a lively social calendar: intimate dinner parties, trips to Ascot, Henley and Glyndebourne, and 'break-away' weekends at the best hotels 'in every corner of the UK'.

If you haven't got £86.25, or the desire to invest

quite so heavily in a potential marriage partner, homelier services are available:

My Bureau is only interested in your need for friendship. I do not ask for fabulous fees to spend on fancy headed paper. The Bureau is run like my housekeeping thus enabling members to benefit from my saving. It is strictly confidential and the rules and regulations strictly kept. In return I will do my best to find you the friend you are seeking.

The proprietor of this cost-conscious enterprise prescribed the modest fee of a maximum of £10 for twelve months. The questionnaire is simple and straightforward and introductions are arranged anonymously. Another low-priced introduction bureau promises unlimited introductions from a 'VERY LARGE REGISTER (thousands of members)' drawn from all walks of life and all age groups. By joining 'you will be "opening the door" to an exciting, fascinating new way of life, and lasting happiness'.

An interesting distinction between the provincial and the national up-market agencies is that the former usually include a sample of anonymous pen portraits of members couched in simple formulae in which a youthful appearance is not infrequently cited as a recommendation for middle-aged members. Here are a few examples:

LADY — 35, 5′ 4″, slim, blonde, attractive . . . wishes to meet intelligent home-loving man, 35—40, who is fit and strong, tall, kind, generous'.

ROBINSON CRUSOE — 41, medium build, 5′ 9″, clean shaven with own hair, youthful appearance and nature.

Yet another nationwide service for singles is provided by Dateline, the computer dating agency. Their sophisticated brochure testifies to the contemporary appeal of computer dating: single people now pose a challenge to a society which creates for many a loneliness it is only possible to remedy through a process of computer matching. The aim of this process is to produce 'compatible matches' — 'a pair of people who have a high probability of being mutually attracted'. Dateline in its latest brochure claims to have 80,000 members, nationwide:

Everyone is affected by the speed and pressures of modern life and that's why men and women of all ages, from every walk of life and all areas of Britain have written to Dateline and have moved on to a new, more fulfilling and stimulating lifestyle. Everyone can and does join Dateline — the only qualification you need is to be single.

Dateline makes available to members a number of potential contacts drawn from all over the British Isles. Thanks to the invention of the computer, men and women need not be at the mercy of the local marriage market or an unfavourable ratio between the sexes. As one satisfied Dateline client testified 'Marriages are made in computers . . . thanks to Dateline International'.

Clearly computer dating, introduction bureaux, and singles clubs can be used for other purposes than those for which they are overtly intended. Not all who participate are looking for a permanent marriage partner. But clients do share membership of a sexual common market where the presentation of an acceptable self-image is just as vital as for swingers and

173

swappers. Thus *Select* magazine, published by Singles Scene Ltd, and linked with Dateline, carries several pages of classified small personal advertisements for the self and a good proportion of those submitted by middle-aged readers emphasize slimness and attractiveness:

SINCERE, slim man, 43, wishes uncomplicated, caring relationship, intelligent, slim, humourous, kind woman. Mutual rapport essential.

WELL TRAVELLED woman, 5 ft 5 in, slim, attractive, divorced, seeks intelligent, well spoken, professional man, probably graduate, for friendship, marriage.

And the trend shows no signs of letting up. *The Daily Star*, a tabloid intent on building up a popular readership to compete with *The Sun* and the *Mirror*, now runs a 'Lonely Hearts' page every Wednesday offering readers the opportunity to 'meet others with similar dispositions'. Maggie Goodheart claims that 'Hundreds of readers have already taken advantage of this special service'. Here is just one hopeful:

SCOTLAND. Refined 1933 female Scorpio, one present careless owner, presentable carriage, good lines, seeks similar gentleman for occasional outings in or around Edinburgh.

Still further variations on this theme can be found in the 'Lonely Hearts' small ad columns of the London magazine *Time Out*, where there is a 'Dating Services' section advertising 'Astromatch' ('Meet astrologically compatible friends/partners'); 'Psychosocial Matching' ('a superior technique which will find just your kind of person . . . scientifically based yet highly personal'); 'Gayway' ('the largest established personal dating service for gay men/bisexuals/lesbians') and a 'Unique Asian Bureau'. Typical examples from the 'Lonely Hearts' section include:

THE IMPOSSIBLE! Beautiful, feminine, educated woman, thirties, used to high standard living seeking stable fulfilled future.

I AM AFFLUENT, SUCCESSFUL MAN, forties, enjoy business, sport, art, travel, children. Genuine plea for responsible, giving, caring relationship. Photo essential for reply.

ICE MAIDEN WANTS THAW. Virgo female, slim, pretty, 5' 6", isolated Midlands, mobile, seeks tall, kind male, 50+, bookish country lover, warmth, humour, mutual defrost.

The systematic search for partners offers additional confirmation of the growing significance of the new images of middle age. As in the world of swingers and swappers, youth, fitness and beauty are keys to success in this particular market place. *Select*, the singles magazine, contains advice on personal grooming and appearance. The issue for November 1980 included a 'before and after' hairstyle feature. And, even more significantly, a letter from a female reader:

Growing Old together: You have published quite a lot of letters recently on the subject of age and relationships. And of course the 'older woman syndrome' has been well documented just about everywhere with all kinds of justifications for the situation — particularly the one about women tending to live longer than men. But there is one aspect of age which nobody seems to have mentioned which is perhaps particularly relevant to your magazine which spends most of its time trying to get people together. And let's face it most of those people are not looking just to expand their social life. Most of them — no matter what they might say — are looking for a permanent partner. But in my experience ageing accelerates enormously with the strains of a permanent relationship. However happy it may be there is something about a partnership which ages people — maybe it's having to worry about something other than one's own needs.

This anxious correspondent was referred to a two-page spread where readers could, by answering twenty questions, solve the pressing problem: 'How Fast Are *You* Growing Old?' Nine out of the twenty questions related to physical changes in skin, hair, weight, and teeth. In addition, there were questions on memory, stress, attitudes, and activities together with 'How active is your sex life?' and 'How much attention do you still pay to dress and posture?' Points out of ten were awarded on each query, and the highest possible score was 200.

If you honestly reached a total of 120 or more, then you can congratulate yourself on clearly not growing old too fast, but also on being well aware of the main pitfalls of ageing. Those who scored under 120 need to ponder again the various points raised — and act accordingly before it is too late!

So, in conclusion, and for the benefit of those of our readers who did not have the opportunity to complete the 'Select' questionnaire, we have devised one of our own which can be found at the end of this book.

Bibliography

Place of publication, unless otherwise stated, is London.

Fiction

A. Alvarez, *Hunt*, Macmillan, 1978

K. Amis, *Jakes's Thing*, Hutchinson, 1978

N. Bawden, *A Woman of My Age*, Penguin, Harmondsworth, 1974

N. Bawden, *Afternoon of a Good Woman*, Penguin, Harmondsworth, 1979

J. Braine, *The Crying Game*, Eyre & Spottiswoode, 1968

J. Braine, *Stay with Me till Morning*, Eyre Methuen, 1970

Colette, *Chéri*, Secker & Warburg, 1963

J. Collins, *Sunday Simmons and Charley Brick*, Sphere, 1973

J. Collins, *Lovers and Gamblers*, Pan, 1978

M. Drabble, *The Ice Age*, Penguin, Harmondsworth, 1978

M. Frayn, *Towards the End of the Morning*, Collins, 1967

B. Glanville, *The Comic*, Secker & Warburg, 1974

J. Haber, *The Users*, Futura, 1978

R. Haley, *Saxby for God*, Arrow Books, 1975

A. Hellman, *Centrefold*, Corgi, 1979

H. Hesse, *Demian*, Harper & Row, New York, 1965

E. Kazan, *The Arrangement*, Collins, 1967

S. Kern, *Fifty*, NEL, 1977

D. Lessing, *The Summer before the Dark*, Cape, 1973

W. Somerset Maugham, *The Moon and Sixpence*, Penguin, Harmondsworth, 1971

D. Nobbs, *The Fall and Rise of Reginald Perrin*, Penguin, Harmondsworth, 1976

D. Nobbs, *The Return of Reginald Perrin*, Penguin, Harmondsworth, 1977

D. Nobbs, *The Better World of Reginald Perrin*, Penguin, Harmondsworth, 1979

B. Norman, *A Series of Defeats*, Quartet, 1977

G. Orwell, *Coming up for Air*, first published 1939, reprinted Secker & Warburg/Octopus, 1976

M. Parkin, *Fast and Loose*, Star, 1980

L. Thomas, *Tropic of Ruislip*, Eyre Methuen, 1974

S. Vizinczey, *In Praise of Older Women*, Pan, 1967

T. Williams, *The Roman Spring of Mrs Stone*, New English Library, 1957

Non Fiction

M. Abrams, 'How and Why We Spend Our Money', in E. Butterworth & D. Weir (eds), *The Sociology of Modern Britain*, Fontana, 1970

M. Abrams, 'Age and Generation', in P. Barker (ed.), *A Sociological Portrait*, Penguin, Harmondsworth, 1973

L. Aldebaran, 'Fat Liberation — A Luxury?', *State and Mind*, June/July, 1977

F.L. Allen, *Only Yesterday* (2 vols), Pelican, Harmondsworth, 1938

W. Anderson, *Gauguin's Paradise Lost*, Viking Press, New York, 1971

K. Anspach, *The Why of Fashion*, Iowa State University Press, Ames, Iowa, 1967

R. Armes, *Film and Reality: An Historical Survey*, Penguin, Harmondsworth, 1974

The Art of being Beautiful, Henry J. Drane, 1902

B. Averon, *Ah Men: What Do Men Want: A Panorama on the Male Crisis*, A & N, New York, 1980

G.R. Bach, 'Creative Exits: Fight Therapy for Divorcees', in V. Franks (ed.), *Women in Therapy*, Brunner/Mazel, New York, 1974

J.O. Balswick & C.W. Peck, 'The Inexpressive Male: A Tragedy of American Society', in A. & J. Skolnick (eds) *Intimacy, Family and Society*, Little, Brown & Co., Boston, 1974

Bamford's Saucy Postcard Annual, Pan, 1976

The Second Bamforth's Saucy Postcard Annual, Pan, 1977

J. Batten, *The Complete Jogger*, Harcourt, Brace, Jovanovich, New York, 1977

C. Beaton, *The Glass of Fashion*, Weidenfeld & Nicolson, 1954

S. de Beauvoir, *Old Age*, Penguin, Harmondsworth, 1977

P. Berger & B. Berger, *Sociology: A Biographical Approach*, Basic Books, New York, 1972

D. Bell, *The Cultural Contradictions of Capitalism*, Heinemann, 1976

A. Scott Beller, *Fat and Thin: A Natural History of Obesity*, Farrer, Strauss & Giroux, New York, 1977

E. Berne, *Games People Play: The Psychology of Human Relationships*, Penguin, Harmondsworth, 1968

P. Bleuel, *Strength through Joy: Sex and Society in Nazi Germany*, Pan, 1976

D. Bowskill, *Swingers and Swappers*, Star, 1975

D. Bowskill & A. Linacre, *The 'Male' Menopause*, Muller, 1976

N. Branson & M. Heinemann, *Britain in the Nineteen Thirties*, Weidenfeld & Nicolson, 1971

M. Brenton, *The American Male: A Penetrating Look at the Masculinity Crisis*, Allen & Unwin, 1966

A. Brien, *Domes of Fortune*, Quartet, 1979

J. Brophy, *The Human Face*, Harrap, 1945

J. Brophy, *Body and Soul*, Harrap, 1948

P. Brown & C. Faulder, *Treat Yourself to Sex: A Guide to Good Loving*, Dent, 1977

K. Brownlow with J. Kobal, *Hollywood: The Pioneers*, Collins, 1979

H. Brüch, *The Importance of Overweight*, Norton, New York, 1957

H. Brüch, *Eating Disorders: Obesity, Anorexia Nervosa and the Person Within*, Routledge & Kegan Paul, 1974

J. Burnett, *Plenty and Want: A Social History of Diet in England from 1875 to the Present Day*, Penguin, Harmondsworth, 1968

R.B. Burns, *The Self Concept: Theory, Measurement, Development and Behaviour*, Longman, 1979

R.N. Butler, 'The Facade of Chronological Age: An Interpretive Summary', *American Journal of Psychiatry*, vol. 119, 1962–3

P. Byrde, *The Male Image: Men's Fashions in Britain 1300–1900*, Batsford, 1979

W.J. Cahman, 'The Stigma of Obesity', *Sociological Quarterly*, vol. 9, 1968

A. Calder-Marshall, *Wish You Were Here: The Art of Donald McGill*, Hutchinson, 1966

M.R.A. Caplin, *Health and Beauty: Or Corsets and Clothing in Accordance with the Physiological Laws of the Human Body*, Darton, (n.d.)

E. Carlton, *Sexual Anxiety: A Study of Male Impotence*, Martin Robertson, Oxford, 1980

D. Carroll, *Four's Company*, Mayflower, 1973

T. King Chambers, *Corpulence*, Longman, Brown, Green and Longmans, 1850

T. King Chambers, *A Manual of Diet in Health and Disease*, Smith, Elder & Co, 1875

F. Le Gros Clarke (ed.), *National Fitness: A Brief Essay on Contemporary Britain*, Macmillan, 1938

M. Clarke & B.G. Anderson, *Culture and Ageing: An Anthropological Study of Older Americans*, Thomas, Springfield, Illinois, 1967

C. Cockburn, *The Devil's Decade*, Sidgwick & Jackson, 1973

B. Coe & P. Yates, *The Snapshot Photograph: The Rise of Popular Photography 1888–1939*, Ash & Grant, 1977

M. Colmer, *Whalebone to See-through: A History of Body Packaging*, Johnston & Bacon, London & Edinburgh, 1979

A. Comfort, *A Good Age*, Mitchell-Beazley, 1977

S. Conran, *Futures*, Sidgwick & Jackson, 1979

F. Conway & J. Siegelman, *Snapping: America's Epidemic of Sudden Personality Change*, Lippincott, Philadelphia, 1978

K. Cooper, *The New Aerobics*, Bantam, New York, 1978

181

R. Corson, *Fashions in Make-up*, Peter Owen, 1972

R. Corson, *Fashions in Hair: The First Five Thousand Years*, Peter Owen, 1965

A.F. Currier, *The Menopause*, Appleton, New York, 1897

C.N. Degler, 'What Ought to Be and What Was: Women's Sexuality in the Nineteenth Century', *American Historical Review*, December 1974

R.M. Deutsch, *The Nuts among the Berries: An Exposé of America's Food Fads*, Ballantine, New York, 1961

A. Disney, 'Where the Dream Comes True', *Observer Magazine*, 13 May 1979

F. Engels, *The Condition of the Working Class in England*, Panther, 1969

E.H. Erikson, *Childhood and Society*, Penguin, Harmondsworth, 1965

S. Ewen, *Captains of Consciousness: Advertising and the Social Roots of Consumer Culture*, McGraw-Hill, New York, 1976

H.J. Eysenck & G. Wilson, *The Psychology of Sex*, Dent, 1979

S. Fawkes, *In Praise of Younger Men*, Hamlyn, 1979

M. Featherstone, Review of D. Levinson *et al.*, 'Seasons of a Man's Life', *Journal of Biosocial Science*, June 1979

M. Featherstone & M. Hepworth, 'Changing Images of Middle Age', in M. Johnson (ed.), *Transitions in Middle and Later Life*, British Society of Gerontology, 1980

J. Fisher, *George Formby*, Woburn-Futura, 1975

M. Fiske, *Middle Age: The Prime of Life?*, Harper & Row, 1979

J.F. Fix, *The Complete Book of Running*, Random House. New York, 1977

J. Scott Francher, 'It's the Pepsi Generation . . . Accelerated Ageing and the Television Commercial', *International Journal of Ageing and Human Development*, vol. 4, no. 3, 1973

H. Franks, *Prime Time*, Pan, 1981

F. Fransella & K. Frost, *On Being a Woman*, Tavistock, 1977

B. Fried, *The Middle Age Crisis*, Harper & Row, New York, 1976

I. Friese, *Women and Sex Roles: A Social Psychological Perspective*, Norton, New York, 1978

E. Fuchs, *The Second Season*, Anchor, New York, 1977

M. Gabor, *The Pin-Up: A Modest History*, Pan, 1973

R. Galella, *Offguard: A Paparazzo Look at the Beautiful People*, McGraw-Hill, 1976

L. Garafola, 'Hollywood and the Myth of the Working Class', *Radical America*, vol. 14, no. 1, 1980

B.B. Gardner, 'The Awakening of Blue Collar Women', *Intellectual Digest*, March 1974

A. Gernsheim, *Fashion and Reality*, Faber & Faber, 1963

H. Gillies & R. Millard, *The Principles and Art of Plastic Surgery*, Butterworth, 1957

E.V. Gillon, (ed.) *The Gibson Girl and Her America: The Best Drawings of Charles Dana Gibson*, Dover, New York, 1969

B. Glover & J. Shepherd, *The Runner's Handbook: A Complete Fitness Guide for Men and Women on the Run*, Penguin, Harmondsworth, 1978

R. Graves & A. Hodge, *The Long Week-End*, Faber & Faber, 1940

B. Green, *I've Lost My Little Willie: A Celebration of Comic Postcards*, Elm Tree/Arrow, 1976

J.A. Greenwald, *Be the Person you were Meant to Be: Antidotes to Toxic Living*, Simon & Schuster, New York, 1974

L.J. Grold, 'Middle Aged, Middle Class Dropouts', *Modern Medicine*, 26 November 1979

R. Hall (ed.), *Dear Dr Stopes: Sex in the 1920s*, Deutsch, 1978

F. Harrison, *The Dark Angel: Aspects of Victorian Sexuality*, Fontana, 1979

J.F.C. Harrison, *The Early Victorians 1832–1851*, Weidenfeld & Nicolson 1971

W. Harvey, *On Corpulence in Relation to Disease*, Henry Renshaw, 1872

M. Haskell, *From Reverence to Rape: The Treatment of Women in the Movies*, NEL, 1975

M. Hepworth & M. Featherstone, 'Going Missing', in R.V. Bailey & J. Young (eds), *Contemporary Social Problems in Britain*, Saxon House, Farnborough, 1973

M. Hepworth & M. Featherstone, ' "Persons Believed Missing": The Search for a Sociological Interpretation', in P. Rock and M. McIntosh (eds), *Deviance and Social Control*, Tavistock, 1974

B. Herndon, *Mary Pickford and Douglas Fairbanks*, W.H. Allen, 1978

C. Hix, *Looking Good: A Guide for Men*, Angus & Robertson, 1979

R. Hoggart, *The Uses of Literacy*, Chatto & Windus, 1957

F.A. Hornibrook, *The Culture of the Abdomen: The Cure of Obesity and Constipation*, Heinemann, 1924

B. & M. Hunt, *Prime Time: A Guide to the Pleasures and Opportunities of the New Middle Age*, Stein & Day, New York, 1975

E. Jaques, 'Death and the Mid Life Crisis', *International Journal of Psychoanalysis*, October 1965

S.A. Kaufman, *The Ageless Woman: Menopause, Hormones and the Quest for Youth*, Prentice-Hall, Englewood Cliffs, New Jersey, 1967

R. Kent, *Aunt Agony Advises: Problem Pages through the Ages*, W.H. Allen, 1979

S. Kern, *Anatomy and Destiny: A Cultural History of the Human Body*, Bobbs-Merrill, New York, 1975

J. Koffend, *A Letter to My Wife*, Saturday Review Press, New York, 1972

R. König, *The Restless Image: A Sociology of Fashion*, Allen & Unwin, 1973

M. Krantzler, *Creative Divorce: A New Opportunity for Personal Growth*, Evans, New York, 1973

J. Kurland, 'Promiscuity in Middle Aged Man', *Medical Aspects of Human Sexuality*, vol. 11, no. 2, 1977

T. Lake & A. Hills, *Affairs: The Anatomy of Extra-Marital Relationships*, Open Books, 1979

K. Lance, *Running for Health and Beauty: A Complete Guide For Women*, Bantam, 1978

L. Langer, *The Importance of Wearing Clothes*, Constable, 1959

C. Lasch, *The Culture of Narcissism: American Life in an Age of Diminishing Expectations*, Norton, New York, 1979

F. Lawrence, *The Easy Guide to Everyday Fitness and Successful Jogging*, Dewynters, 1978

M.W. Lear, 'Is There a Male Menopause?', *New York Times Magazine*, 28 January 1973

M. Levin (ed.), *Hollywood and the Great Fan Magazines*, Arbor House, New York, 1970

L. Levine & B. Doherty, *The Menopause*, Random House, New York, 1952

D.J. Levinson, C. Darrow, R. Klein, M.H. Levinson & B. McKee, *The Seasons of a Man's Life*, Knopf, New York, 1978

L.S. Lewis & D. Brisset, 'Sex as Work' in E.C. McDonagh & J.E. Simpson (eds) *Social Problems: Persistent Challenges*, Holt, Rinehart & Winston, New York, 1969

J. Lillerfors, *Total Running*, Morrow, New York, 1979

M. Lippa & D. Newton, *The World of Small Ads*, Hamlyn, 1979

A. Lorand, *Old Age Deferred: The Causes of Old Age and Its Postponement by Hygienic and Therapeutic Measures*, Davis, Philadelphia, 1922

J.A. Lucas, 'The "Alternative Life-Style" of Playboys and Playmates', *The New York Times Magazine*, 11 June, 1972

R. & H. Lynd, *Middletown*, Harcourt & Brace, 1929

J. McCabe, *Mr. Laurel and Mr. Hardy*, Signet, New York, 1966

P.M. McGrady, *The Youth Doctors*, Barker, 1969

F.C. MacGregor, *Transformation and Identity: The Face and Plastic Surgery*, Quadrangle, New York, 1974

R.M. MacIver, *The Challenge of the Passing Years: My Encounter with Time*, Simon & Schuster, New York, 1962

M. Maltz, *Evolution of Plastic Surgery*, Froben Press, New York, 1946

M. Maltz, *New Faces, New Futures: Rebuildilng Character with Plastic Surgery*, R.R. Smith, New York, 1936

Man's Body: An Owner's Manual, Paddington Press, 1976

G. Maranan, *The Climacteric (The Critical Age)*, Henry Klimpton, 1929

S. Mathews, 'Old Women and Identity Maintenance', *Urban Life*, October 1975

N. Mayer, *The Male Mid-Life Crisis*, Signet, New York, 1978

The Middle Years, TV Publications, 1967

D.T. Miller & M. Novak, *The Fifties: The Way We Really Were*, Doubleday, New York, 1975

L. Miller, *Late Bloom: New Lives for Women*, Paddington Press, 1979

H. Miner, 'Body Ritual among the Nacirema', *American Anthropologist*, 58, 1956

T. Morgan, *Somerset Maugham*, Cape, 1980

F. Moriarty, *True Confessions: 1918–1979*, Simon & Schuster, New York, 1979

E. Morin, *The Stars*, Grove Press, New York, 1960

S. Morini, *Body Sculpture: Plastic Surgery from Head to Toe*, Delacorte Press, New York, 1969

Z. Moss, 'It Hurts to Be Alive and Obsolete: The Ageing Woman', in R. Morgan (ed.) *Sisterhood is Powerful*, Vintage, New York, 1970

B.L. Neugarten & N. Datan, 'The Middle Years', in S. Arieti (ed.), *American Handbook of Ageing*, Vol. 1, Basic Books, New York, 1974

B.L. Neugarten, 'Age Groups in American Society and the Rise of the Young Old', *Annals of The American Academy of Political and Social Science*, September 1974

J. Nidetch, *The Story of Weight Watchers*, Signet, New York, 1979

G. Nuttall & R. Carmichael, *Common Factors/Vulgar Factions*, Routledge & Kegan Paul, 1977

N. & G. O'Neill, *Shifting Gears*, Evans, New York, 1974

S. Orbach, *Fat is a Feminine Issue: The Anti-Diet Guide to Permanent Weight Loss*, Paddington Press, 1978

G. Orwell, 'The Art of Donald McGill', *Horizon*, February 1942, reprinted in *The Collected Essays, Journalism and Letters of George Orwell*, Vol. 2, *My Country Right or Left, 1940–43*, Penguin, Harmondsworth, 1970

V. Packard, *The Hidden Persuaders*, Longmans, Green, 1957

F.S. Perls, *In and out of the Garbage Pail*, Bantam, New York, 1972

K. Perutz, *Beyond the Looking Glass: Life in the Beauty Culture*, Penguin, Harmondsworth, 1972

M.C. Phillips, *Skin Deep: The Truth about Beauty Aids — Safe and Harmful*, Vanguard Press, New York, 1934

D. Piper, *The English Face*, Thames & Hudson, 1957

W.B. Pitkin, *Life Begins At Forty*, McGraw-Hill, New York & London, 1932

Pont, *The British Character*, Fontana, 1956

J.B. Priestley, *English Journey* (first published 1934), reprinted Penguin, Harmondsworth, 1977

M. Puner, *To the Good Long Life: What We Know about Growing Old*, Macmillan, 1978

J.W. Ramsey, 'Alternative Life-Styles', *Society*, July/August 1977

C. Rayner, *Everything Your Doctor Would Tell You If He Had the Time*, Pan, 1980

C. Stanford Read, *Fads and Feeding*, Methuen, 1908

H. Reid, 'American Social Science in the Politics of Time and the Crises of Technocorporate Society', *Politics and Society*, vol. 3, no. 2, 1973

R. Reitz, *Menopause: A Positive Approach*, Harvester Press, 1979

D. Riesman, N. Glazer & R. Denney, *The Lonely Crowd: A Study of the Changing American Character*, Doubleday, New York, 1953

P. Roberts, *The Swapping Game*, Everest, 1976

D. Robinson, *Hollywood in the Twenties*, Zwemmer, 1968

J. Rockwell, 'Big is not Beautiful', *New Society*, 22 June 1976

M.E. Roch, K. Rogers & J.B. Eichler, *Dress, Adornment and Social Order*, Wiley, New York, 1965

M. Rosen, *Popcorn Venus: Women, Movies and the American Dream*, Coward, McCann & Gergeshan, New York, 1972

D. Rosenblatt & E.A. Suchman, 'The Underutilisation of Medical-Care Services by Blue-collarites', in A.B. Shostak and W. Gomberg (eds), *Blue Collar World*, Prentice-Hall, Englewood Cliffs, New Jersey, 1964

A. Rosenfeld, *Prolongevity*, Knopf, New York, 1976

L.C. Rosten, *Hollywood: The Movie Colony, the Movie Makers*, Harcourt, Brace & Co., New York, 1941

E.A. Rout, *Restoration Exercises for Women*, Heinemann, 1925

I. Rubin, *Forever Thin*, Bernard Geis Associates, 1970

J. Rubin, *Growing (Up) at Thirty-seven*, Evans, New York, 1976

J. Rubin, *Do It: Scenarios of the Revolution*, Simon & Schuster, New York, 1970

L. Rubin, *Women of a Certain Age: The Midlife Search for Self*, Harper & Row, New York, 1979

H. Rubinstein, *The Art of Feminine Beauty*, Horace Liveright, New York, 1930

B. Rudofsky, *The Unfashionable Human Body*, Hart-Davis, 1972

H.J. Ruebsaat & R. Hull, *The Male Climacteric*, Hawthorn, New York, 1975

M. Scarf, 'He and She', *New York Times Magazine*, 7 May 1972

D. Scully & P. Bart, 'A Funny Thing Happened on the Way to the Orifice: Women in Gynaecology Text Books', in J. Huber (ed.), *Changing Women in a Changing Society*, Chicago University Press, Chicago, 1973

J.T. Shackleton, *The Golden Age of the Railway Poster*, NEL, 1976

E. Le Shan, *The Wonderful Crisis of Middle Age*, Warner, New York, 1974

E.M. Schur, *The Awareness Trap: Self Absorption Instead of Social Change*, Quadrangle, New York, 1976

G. Sheehy, *Passages: Predictable Crisis of Adult Life*, Corgi, 1977

J.V. Shoemaker, *Health and Beauty*, F.A. Davis, Philadelphia, 1908

A. Shostak, 'Middle Aged Working Class Americans at Home', *Occupational Mental Health*, vol. 2, 1972

A.W. Simon, *The New Years: A New Middle Age*, Gollancz, 1968

J.W. Smith & S. Sinclair Baker, *Doctor Make Me Beautiful*, David McKay & Co., New York, 1973

R. Smith, *The Dieter's Guide to Weight Loss during Sex*, Workman Pub, New York, 1978

S. Sontag, *On Photography*, Allen Lane, 1978

A.W. Spence, 'The Male Climacteric: Is It an Entity?', *British Medical Journal*, vol. 6, 1954

D. Spoto, *Camarado: Hollywood and the American Man*, Plume, New York, 1978

G. Squire, *Dress, Art and Society 1566–1970*, Studio Vista, 1974

C. Stainsby (ed.), *Strip Jack Naked*, Gentry, 1972

S. Stall, *What a Man of Forty-five Ought to Know*, Vir, 1901

P. Stallings with H. Mandelbaum, *Flesh and Fantasy*, Macdonald & Janes, 1978

D.E. Stannard, 'Growing up and Growing Old: Dilemmas of Ageing in Bureaucratic America', in S.F. Spiker, K.M. Woodward and D.D. Van Tassel (eds), *Ageing and the Elderly*, Humanities Press, New York, 1978

P.N. Stearns, *Old Age in European Society: The Case of France*, Croom Helm, 1977

M. Stopes, *Change of Life in Men and Women*, Putnam, 1936

D. Sudnow, *Passing On: The Social Organisation of Dying*, Prentice-Hall, Englewood Cliffs, New Jersey, 1967

G. Talese, *Thy Neighbour's Wife*, Collins, 1980

C. Temple, *Jogging for Fitness and Pleasure*, Sunday Times/ World's Work, 1977

E.P. Thompson, 'Time, Work Discipline and Industrial Capitalism', *Past and Present*, December 1967

A. Tolson, *The Limits of Masculinity*, Tavistock, 1977

G. Tuchman, A.K. Daniels & J. Benét, *Hearth and Home:*

Images of Woman in the Mass Media, Oxford University Press, New York, 1978

B. Tulloh, *The Complete Jogger*, Macmillan, 1979

E.S. Turner, *The Shocking History of Advertising*, Joseph, 1952

S.A. Voak, *Looking Good*, Macdonald, 1978

A. Walker, *Stardom: The Hollywood Phenomenon*, Stein & Day, New York, 1970

M. Walters, *The Nude Male: A New Perspective*, Paddington Press, New York & London, 1978

J.K. Walton, *The Blackpool Landlady: A Social History*, Manchester University Press, Manchester, 1978

J.G. Weightman, 'The Solar Revolution: Reflections on a Theme in French Literature', *Encounter*, December 1970

B. Weston, *Weight Watchers: A Way of Life*, Hamlyn, 1975

C.L. White, *Women's Magazines 1693–1968*, Joseph, 1970

D. White, 'The Pursuit of "Nature" ', *New Society*, 27 March 1975

L. Williams, *Middle Age and Old Age*, Oxford University Press, Oxford, 1925

G. Wilson & D. Bias, *Love's Mysteries: The Psychology of Sexual Attraction*, Open Books, 1976

R. Wilson, *Feminine Forever*, Evans, New York, 1960

T. Wolfe, 'The Me Decade and the Third Great Awakening', in *Mauve Gloves and Madmen, Clutter and Vine*, Bantam, New York, 1977

T. Wolfe, *In Our Time*: Picador, 1980

P. Wyden, *The Overweight Society: An Authoritative, Entertaining Investigation into the Facts and Follies of Girth Control*, Evans Bros, 1966

L. Yablonsky, *The Extra Sex Factor: Why over Half of America's Men Play Around*, Times Books, New York, 1979

M. Yaffé, 'Inside Every Fat Man . . .', *New Society*, 21 June 1973

B. Zilbergeld, *Man and Sex: A Guide to Sexual Fulfilment*, Fontana, 1980

The Mid-Life Questionnaire

Not to be completed by anyone under 35

Please answer all the questions. All you have to do is tick the appropriate answer and add up your score at the end.

WARNING: this test could damage your self-image.

	Tick	Score
1 How often do you look at your face in the mirror each day?		
all the time		g
frequently		e
seldom		d
only when I have to		c
never		a
2 How many wrinkles can you count?		
absolutely none		g
2 to 10		f
10 to 20		e
20 upwards		d
innumerable		a
3 Is your hair:		
untouched by grey		g
flecked with grey		d
completely grey		b
dyed or tinted		e
4 How would you describe your smile?		
confident		g
exuberant		g
nervous		b
5 When you smile, what colour are your teeth?		
brilliant white		g
off white		d
nicotine brown		a
6 Is your face dangerously flushed?		
never		g
hardly ever		e
perpetually		b

				Tick	Score
7 How many chins have you?	1				g
	1 to 5				e
	5 and over				b
8 When you pinch your cheek is the amount of flesh:	under an inch				g
	between 1 and 5 inches				e
	over 5 inches				b
9 Is your face:	bronzed				g
	pallid				e
10 When you bob up and down does your flesh:	remain firmly in place				g
	wobble up and down like a jelly				b
11 Cast an eye over your shoulder — is your backside:	taut and firm				g
	a thing of beauty and joy forever				g
	rather protuberant				c
	invisible				d
12 Take a good look at yourself — would you feel out of place on a nudist beach?	yes				b
	no				g
13 Does your swimsuit set off your body to advantage?	yes				g
	no				b

	Tick	Score

14 Are your clothes:

up to date		g
1 to 5 years old		e
5 to 10 years old		d
pre-World War II		b
pre-World War I		a

15 When you go to bed do you sleep:

clothed only in your loveliness		g
in erotic glamour wear		g
in pyjamas/nighty		d
in your underwear		b
in bed socks and nightcap		a

16 Do you think you've got:

the right face on the right body		g
the right face on the wrong body		d
the wrong face on the right body		e
a bad deal all round		b

17 As you get older do you think exercise is:

more important		g
moderately important		d
completely unnecessary		a

	Tick	Score
18 Do you use a: fully equipped gymnasium		g
swimming pool		f
weight-training kit		d
exercise cycle		d
squash court		g
rowing machine		d
bullworker		d
yoga mat		e
track suit		e
skipping rope		c
pair of plimsolls		c
box of dominoes		b
set of darts		b
ludo board		a
19 Do you indulge in any of the following anti-health behaviour? smoking		a
drinking		c
sitting		a
not doing anything at all		a
20 How calorie-controlled is your diet? rigorously		g
sporadically		d
have given up hope		a
21 When you stand on the bathroom scales are you: wildly excited		g
mildly amused		d
horrified		b
unable to see the scales		a

		Tick	Score
22 Would you describe yourself as:	sexual dynamite		g
	a swinger		g
	a swapper		g
	a middle aged fantasizer		d
	a voyeur		c
	too tired to bother		b
	someone who can't understand what all the fuss is about		a
23 Is your bedroom a:	gymnasium		g
	playroom		f
	place *strictly* for sleeping		b
	museum		a
24 Do you possess:	erotic glamourwear		g
	a collection of unusual photographs		f
	an up-to-date sex manual		g
	ginseng		d
	one or more (not more than 10) aphrodisiacs		f
	a sex board game		e
	a bored sex partner		a
25 Does your partner:	bring you surprise packets of sexy underwear		g
	like to play exotic love games		g
	frequently complain of a bedtime headache		a

		Tick	Score
26 Hast thou ever coveted thy neighbour's husband/wife?	often		g
	now and again		e
	not since we moved house		d
	never		a
27 What do you think is the ideal age combination for sexual satisfaction?	male aged 17 + female aged 55		g
	male aged 28 + female aged 45		f
	both partners the same age		d
	male aged 45 + female aged 28		e
	male aged 55 + female aged 17		g
28 Do you think your present life is:	beyond your wildest dreams		g
	better than you expected		f
	not quite as bad as you had feared		d
	much the same as before		c
	worse than ever		a
	like living with the brakes on		b
	running out fast		c
29 Are your children a source of:	companionship		e
	competition		a
	envy		a
	anxiety		b
	despair		c

	Tick	Score
30 Have you ever considered: becoming a missing person		e
joining an encounter group		g
having cosmetic surgery		g
buying a copy of *Passages* or *The Wonderful Crisis of Middle Age*		g
none of the above		a
31 Do you believe any of the following statements true? couples grow closer together as they grow older		d
you've only one life to live and you should please yourself		g
life begins at 40		g
you're as old as you féel		d
all you need in middle age is a bit of peace and quiet		b

SCORING

The number of points for each letter
is as follows:

a	=	−5
b	=	0
c	=	1
d	=	2
e	=	3
f	=	4
g	=	5

150 points and over

Congratulations! You are clearly one of the growing number of prime
timers — which means, by all accounts, you will stay young and beautiful
for ever. The maximum score is 244; if you get anywhere near that you
deserve a slap up high calorie dinner — but we know you wouldn't want it.
Why not give the rest of us a chance and go on a crash diet of brown ale
and black pudding.

50–150 points

Like most of us you're a survivor. You're aware of the new image of
middle age but value your appearance and health, not, however, to the
exclusion of everything else. Some days you feel young, some days you
feel old. You'll try anything once but would much prefer not to spend
your life in front of a mirror.

50 points and under

The lowest score you could possibly get is −94. If you came anywhere
close to this figure you probably can't see what all the fuss is about; but
beware, some experts believe you're an endangered species. You are not
entitled to the high calorie dinner (much as you would enjoy it); keep right
on to the end of the road!

Index

Abrams, Mark   16
advertising, influence of   69, 78,
    80—1, 86—7, 90; *see also* media
ageing: and character changes
    11—12, 43; physical signs of
    1—14, 16—17, 50, 55—6,
    60—1, 66—7, 93—4, 112—13,
    126, 129; social aspects of
    3, 17, 93, 95
Alvarez, A.   11
'Aphrodite complex'   30, 34;
    see also men, older, and
    younger women
appearance: changes in   14,
    54—5, 163; emphasis on   xii,
    1—5, 10—11, 22, 52—3, 62—5,
    67, 69—70, 78—80, 90,
    110—11, 127—9, 131—2, 135,
    175; and fitness   93, 97,
    100—1, 107, 115, 118—19,
    124, 159, 165
attitudes towards middle age   xi,
    1, 22, 69—70, 86; negative
    5—7, 12—13, 91; positive   25,
    44—5, 94, 154, 156

Bakewell, Joan   26—7
beauty: emphasis on   25, 59—60,
    66; and fitness   94—5, 104,
    107, 112, 120—3, 136, 159,
    169, 175; and Hollywood
    75—8, 86, 90; idealized
    standards of   xi, 3, 69—70,
    94—5
beauty contests   86
Beauvoir, Simone de   7
Beerbohm, Max   67—8
Berger, B., and Berger, P.   6
body: consciousness of   9—11,
    56, 69, 80—6, 110, 114—15,
    121, 167; maintenance   11,
    53, 55, 94—5, 112—13, 125,
    159
Bowskill, D., and Linacre, A.
    37—8
Brophy, John   1—2
Brown, P., and Faulder, Carolyn
    138—9, 140—1

Calder-Marshall, Arthur   56
Caplin, M.R.A.   59
Castle, Roy   96—7
Chambers, Thomas King   56—8
Collins, Jackie   8—9, 165
Collins, Joan   27, 91—2
Conran, Shirley   7, 14, 22
Conway, F., and Siegelmann, J.
    169—70
corsetry: for men   64—6; for
    women   59, 61, 64, 135—6

201

cosmetic surgery 70, 75, 80–1,
   125–35; for men 132–3;
   for women 166
cosmetics 6, 69–71, 75, 127;
   for men 68, 80–1; for
   women 59–60, 67–8, 71–3,
   76–80, 92, 129

Datan, Nancy 47
Dawson, Ronald 153
death, awareness of 42, 50, 163
Dors, Diana 19
Drabble, Margaret 4–5
Drake, Charlie 93
'Dream' 46–7, 49, 51, 164

'empty nest syndrome' 15–16,
   42, 45–6, 154
est (Erhardt Seminar Training)
   158, 166–8, 170

Fairbanks, Douglas 73, 75, 83,
   92, 102
Fawkes, Sandy 26
fitness: emphasis on 5–6,
   10–11, 52–3, 58, 61–4, 66,
   92–109, 110–13, 136, 155–6,
   159, 169, 175; hiking 88–9;
   and Hollywood 73, 75–6,
   78–9, 81, 83, 86, 88–9, 90,
   166–7; idealized standards of
   xi, 69; see also health; jogging;
   sex; youth
Fontaine, Lynn 71
Foster, Brendan 102–3
Frayn, Michael 16
Friese, Irene 16–17

Gauguin, Paul 49–50, 161–2
glamourwear: for men 150; for
   women 147–9

Glover, B., and Shepherd, J.
   105–6
Greenwald, J. 157–8

Haley, R. 12
Hall, Unity 21–2, 31, 52, 99
Harvey, William 58
Haskell, Molly 32
health, concern with 10–11,
   56–66, 95–107, 111, 115,
   120, 154; and Hollywood
   69, 75–6, 79, 82, 87–8;
   see also fitness; jogging
health farms 8, 117–18, 125
Hix, Charles 110–11
Hodgkinson, Liz 24
Hollywood 25, 33, 69–89,
   164–6; and cosmetics
   69–73; and cult of youth
   73–8, 82, 86, 90; see also
   beauty; fitness; health
Hormone Replacement Therapy
   (HRT) 19–20, 25
Hornibrook, F.A., and
   Hornibrook, E. 61–2, 64,
   66
Hunt, B., and Hunt, M. 154–5,
   160

introduction agencies 170–3

Jacks, Brian 100
James, Clive 94
Jaques, Elliot 40
jogging 52, 93, 101–9, 111

Kazan, Elia 31–2
Keith, Arthur 63
Kern, Seymour 7–8
Kinney, Jean 45
Koffend, John 162–4
Kurland, Judith 35

202

Lawrence, Freddie 97—9, 106
Le Shan, E. 44, 156
Levinson, Daniel 43—4, 46—7, 164
lonely hearts columns 174—5
Lorand, Arthur 67

Maugham, W. Somerset 13, 49, 161—2
Mayer, N. 32—3, 44, 160—1
media: and attitudes to ageing 5—6, 17—18, 24, 53, 159, 164; and attitudes to menopause 35—8, 41; see also advertising
men: and appearance xii, 7—8, 14, 26—7; older, and younger women 25, 29—35, 37, 114, 154; and sex drive 23—4, 25, 33, 39; see also menopause, male
menopause, female 19—28, 46; see also sex
menopause, male 14, 29—39, 40—1, 51—2, 158
Merrifield, Mary P. 60
middle age, definitions of 14, 43, 60, 67, 75
middle age, images of: new xi—xii, 16, 27—8, 53, 76—7, 159—60, 164, 175; traditional 55, 113, 154
middle-age spread xi, 6, 14, 52—3, 55, 58, 62, 65, 87—8, 96; see also weight
mid-life crisis xi, 14, 34, 40—53, 156—7; for men 40—1, 46, 48—9, 160—1, 163—4; for women 41—2, 45—6, 164, 169; see also self-actualization
Miner, Horace 10

mirror: as reminder of ageing 4—5, 9—10, 13, 77—8; and sex 148
Moore, Dudley 13—14, 35—6
Moore, Roger 92—3

Neugarten, Bernice 15, 45, 47
Newton, Frank 108
Nicholson, Viv 27
Nidetch, Jean 124
Norman, Barry 5

old age, stereotype of 12—13
O'Neill, N., and O'Neill, G. 155—6
Orwell, George 55

Pickford, Mary 70—1
Priestley, J.B. 72—3, 88—9
Proops, Marje 21, 30, 36—7, 40, 52, 99, 143

Raft, George 25—6
Rayner, Claire 17—18, 22—3, 33—4, 41, 132, 137—8, 146
Reich, Larry 123
Rosten, Leo 73—4
Rout, Ettie 61—4
Rubin, Jerry 158—9, 168
Rubinstein, Helena 76—8, 125—6

self-actualization 43—6, 49—51, 152, 156—64, 166—7; see also mid-life crisis
self-image 22, 69, 95, 166—70, 173—4
sex 137—53, 155, 169; fantasies 146—7, 150, 152; and fitness 94, 104, 107, 111—12, 119, 133, 142—3, 145, 156; and glamour 90—3; and

203

menopause 21–6, 30, 32–3, 39; revitalization of 137–41, 144–5, 147–52; *see also* swinging
sexual aids 145, 148, 150–2
Shann, Rosalie 24–5
Sheehy, G. 42, 44, 51, 157
Shoemaker, John V. 60–1
Shostak, Arthur 48
singles 170–5
slimming 6, 87–8, 99–100, 111–13, 124–5; by men 114, 118, 123; by women 22, 115–22; *see also* middle-age spread; weight
slob, the 97–9, 113
Smith, J.W., and Baker, S. Sinclair 128–9
Smith, Richard 111–12
sunbathing and exposure of the body 82–6
swinging 140, 143–5, 167

Talese, Gay 142–3, 152
Taylor, Elizabeth 116–18, 125
time, approaches to 13–14, 15–16, 44–5, 163
Tulloch, Bruce 104–5

Watson, Lesley 108
weight: increase in 56–66, 87–8, 95–6, 99–100, 107; in men 113; in women 114; *see also* middle-age spread; slimming
White, Cynthia 79
Whitehorn, Katharine 3, 6–7, 131–2
Williams, Leonard 66
Wilson, Robert 20
women: and appearance xii, 6–7, 14; older, and younger men 24–7, 30; and sex-drive 21, 23–6, 29, 30, 33; *see also* menopause, female
Women's League of Health and Beauty 89

youth: emphasis on xi, 1, 3–6, 45, 69, 72–8, 82, 86, 90, 155, 172; and fitness 10–11, 94, 101, 103–5, 107, 112, 120, 136, 145, 159, 169, 175; preservation of 25, 67, 128–9, 133–5